FREDDIE MERCURY
The Great Pretender

INSIGHT
EDITIONS

Insight Editions
PO Box 3088
San Rafael, CA 94912
www.insighteditions.com

First published in the United States in 2012 by Insight Editions.

The Freddie Mercury logo is a trademark of Mercury Songs Limited and is used under licence
Copyright © 2012 Mercury Songs Limited
Design copyright © 2012 Carlton Books Limited
Freddie Mercury logo © 2012 Mercury Song Limited

www.freddiemercury.com

Text: Sean O'Hagan
Captions: Greg Brooks and Phil Symes
Art Direction: Richard Gray

Library of Congress Cataloging-in-Publication Data available.

ISBN: 978-1-60887-178-0

ROOTS of PEACE   REPLANTED PAPER

Insight Editions, in association with Roots of Peace, will plant two trees for each tree used in the
manufacturing of this book. Roots of Peace is an internationally renowned humanitarian organization
dedicated to eradicating land mines worldwide and converting war-torn lands into productive farms
and wildlife habitats. Together, we will plant two million fruit and nut trees in Afghanistan and
provide farmers there with the skills and support necessary for sustainable land use.

Printed in China

10 9 8 7 6 5 4 3 2 1

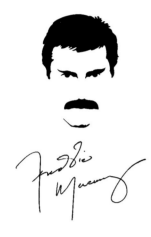

FREDDIE MERCURY
The Great Pretender
A Life in Pictures

INSIGHT 👁 EDITIONS

San Rafael, California

"I won't be a rock star.

I will be a legend!"

INTRODUCTION

It's 8 pm and I am sitting in an edit suite in Soho, London, watching the uncut rushes of Freddie Mercury's infamous birthday party in Munich, 1985. I am lucky enough to be directing a new documentary about my hero.

The film is so clear that I feel that I'm at the party myself. I can taste the champagne, hear the music and smell the PVC. Beneath the disco balls and ultraviolet lighting, amongst the fun, the leather, bare buttocks, moustaches, strippers and Brian May dressed as a witch – is Freddie. It is hard to tell if he is enjoying himself or not. A three-tiered cake is carried across the dance floor by several chefs as the birthday boy is ushered over to blow out the 39 candles. Slightly embarrassed, he blows out a few and retreats into a corner of the room away from everyone, where he spends most of the night.

This is man who performed 'I Want To Break Free' in drag in front of 350,000 fans at the Rock In Rio Festival. The man who sang 'Bohemian Rhapsody' upside-down with the Royal Ballet. The man who stole the show at Live Aid with the whole world watching. Yet being the centre of attention at his own party appears to make him squirm.

Freddie Mercury said he was a man of extremes. On stage he was indestructible. He was Mr Fahrenheit. Off stage he was shy, witty and, according to everyone close to him, the best friend you could ever have.

Freddie Mercury was the Great Pretender.

This party footage in the past has often been used to depict his 'outrageous' personal life. However this wasn't really Freddie's personal life. It's what he wanted us to believe was his personal life, to embellish the image and persona he had created.

Freddie's personal life was very different. Yes he had his fair share of crazy nights out and he was not afraid to admit he was excessive in all areas, but Freddie was also someone who would go to the ballet, the opera and musicals. He collected Japanese art and Koi carp. He was a loyal godfather, rang his cats when he was away from home, played Scrabble and his favourite TV show was *Countdown*.

The real significance of the party was that it was to be the last of its kind. It marked Freddie's farewell to the lifestyle he had been living for five or so years. Freddie was almost forty, the world had woken up to AIDS and things had to change.

From 1979 to 1985, Queen had gone from being the biggest band in Europe to the biggest band in the world. Freddie was living it up in New York and Munich, away from the prying eyes of the British press, where he could be himself. During this time Freddie recorded his first solo album *Mr Bad Guy*. Despite receiving a large advance from CBS the album failed to make an impact, reaching No. 6 in the UK and 159 in the USA. Walter Yetnikoff, Head of CBS, claimed it was the worst record deal he had ever made.

After that party in Munich, Freddie returned to familiar territory, Queen and London. He moved into his dream mansion and the band began work on *A Kind Of Magic* which would be Queen's first UK number one album in six years, followed by their record breaking Magic Tour which ended at Knebworth Park in August 1986.

The band decided to take another long break, but already Freddie was itching to do something new. He was now 40 and wanted a challenge in life. Unfazed by the disappointment of his first solo outing, he was determined to make something "of some note. Not just another bunch of songs," as he put it. He thought about writing a musical and then had the idea of recording an album of cover versions, starting with 'The Great Pretender'. However, that went out of the window when he got a call from one of the world's greatest opera singers.

Flash back six years. It's 1981. Freddie and his personal assistant Peter 'Phoebe' Freestone are sitting in the Royal Opera House, Covent Garden watching Pavarotti in Verdi's *Un Ballo De Maschera*. Freddie loved Pavarotti's voice and admired his control – but then the mezzo-soprano walked on and Freddie was blown away. His jaw dropped and he turned to Peter and said "I have just heard the most beautiful voice in the world." That voice belonged to Montserrat Caballé. Freddie was in awe. Years later on tour with Queen in Barcelona, he was interviewed on TV, and when asked who his favourite singer was he beamed, "You won't believe this but it's Montserrat Caballé … She's just the best!"

When news got back to Montserrat, she invited Freddie to Barcelona to meet. Not only did she agree to record a song, but an entire album. Freddie was in his element. He was working with his heroine and stretching his musical skills into a new dimension. On an emotional level he had finally found happiness with long-term boyfriend Jim Hutton, who had now moved into Garden Lodge. Life couldn't have been better, except Freddie knew he was HIV positive – he had AIDS. He didn't know how long he had to live but what he did know was that the current album he was working on with Montserrat could be his last and he was determined to make it the best.

The critically acclaimed 'Barcelona' single, and album, went on to sell over a million copies and became the official song for the Barcelona '92 Olympic Games. Freddie regrouped with Queen and went back into the studio to record two more albums in quick succession, *The Miracle* and *Innuendo*, completing a fraction of the third, *Made In Heaven*, which the band released in 1995. Freddie was more creative than ever, fuelled by the determination to make great music that would last forever.

Ten days before Freddie died, Jim Beach, the band's manager, met with him to discuss what could be done with his legacy. Freddie quipped, "You can do whatever you like with my image, my music, remix it, re-release it, whatever – just never make me boring."

Over the years Jim Beach and the remaining members of Queen have continued to keep that promise and in 2012, to celebrate 25 years of *Barcelona*, the whole album was re-recorded the way it should have been "had Freddie had the balls to do it at the time." The Eighties keyboard has been replaced with an eighty piece orchestra which lifts what was already an outstanding album into a whole new stratosphere. Rousing, triumphant, emotional and magnificent.

Freddie Mercury continues to capture the hearts, the minds and the ears of everyone who hears his music or watches his videos and concerts. He hated interviews but when he had the right person asking the questions – someone he could trust – he was utterly open, modest, hilarious and charming. Life was for living. Life was for fun. "Fuck tomorrow, it's today, dear."

Twenty-one years after his death, Freddie Mercury is still very much alive. He influences and enlightens new generations of musicians and fans alike. He will always be unique. He will always be the greatest – and he will never, ever be boring.

And now I want to cry.

Rhys Thomas, London, May 2012.

Freddie Mercury

"I SEE A LITTLE SILHOUETTO OF A MAN"

Six months into the new millennium, a period not quite lost in the mists of time, a huge advert appeared decorating various London underground stations. It was for an online investment company called Egg and, somewhat bizarrely, it featured the following lines from 'Bohemian Rhapsody' by Queen.

> *"I see a little silhouetto of a man*
> *Scaramouche scaramouche*
> *Will you do the fandango*
> *Thunderbolt and lightning*
> *Very very frightening me*
> *Galileo Galileo Galileo Galileo Galileo Figaro"*

I recall now that in bigger, bolder, red letters, however, the lingering traveller was also instructed, DO NOT SING THIS! Entrapped by one of the oldest teases in the book – asking you not to do something, while simultaneously encouraging you do it – the viewer's eye was then led to the killer pay-off line – "You may not be able to control yourself, but you can control your investments." Perfect.

The advert managed to be blindingly obvious in its appeal to our base curiosity *and* knowingly clever in the way that post-modern online advertising tends to be. For once, though, the copywriter who thought up this concept deserved the no doubt inflated salary he (or perhaps it was a she) took home, because, on closer inspection, the ad was also clever on a whole other level. First up, it made me – a reluctant tube traveller and an even more reluctant advertising victim – *smile.* And, it made me smile on an overcrowded Tube platform on the Northern line during the morning rush hour. (The reason I smiled, in retrospect, was because the words were already dancing in my head by the time I read the instruction to try not to sing them.)

Secondly, it made me *think* – though not about what the advertisers wanted me to think of (no one, however clever and persuasive they might be, is going to persuade me to ponder the benefits of investment, online or otherwise, on the Northern line in the morning rush hour.) No, what it made me think about was the *specificity* of the choice of song; how some no doubt pony-tailed guy in a chic and minimal advertising office, who was probably even born when Freddie Mercury was writing the lyrics quoted above, had found the perfect, perhaps the only vehicle, for his advertising concept. That vehicle was not even a whole pop song but a snatch, a mere fragment of the greater whole that is 'Bohemian Rhapsody'. A fragment, though, that, once absorbed, remains in the listener's – and, in this case, the viewer's – head, despite all efforts to remove it.

This in turn made me think about pop song lyrics in general, their seemingly effortless ability to lodge themselves in the brain like no other popular art form; their ability to become part not just of one's personal consciousness but of the collective popular consciousness. And, in this particular instance, not just the British, European or American popular consciousness, but the global one. Then, inevitably, I found myself moving from the universal to the particular, thinking specifically about this pop song called 'Bohemian Rhapsody' – though, on one level, of course, it is as far from the traditional idea of the pop song as it is possible to go.

One of the first things that struck me about all this, on a personal level, was the fact that, though it has been lodged firmly in my consciousness, immovable from the first moment I heard it back in 1975, 'Bohemian Rhapsody' was, for most of this time, not even a song I *liked*. In fact, for a long time, during and after the would-be Punk purge of 1976/77, when Queen represented the enemy incarnate, it was a song I actively hated. I saw it as a big, blowsy, pretentious, overblown epic that, like many of its even more big and blowsy and pretentious progressive rock (hereafter referred to as prog-rock) cousins, was exactly the kind of thing I defined my whole pop life *against*. (Since those far-off punk days, of course, I have wised up considerably, and now, having passed through the *knowingly ironic* phase of appreciation for 'Bohemian Rhapsody', I can simply bow to the sheer lunatic genius of the lyrics, the arrangements, the operatic overstatement – though I still, it must be said, retain an abiding aversion to all things prog-rock.)

My ruminations on the singularity of 'Bohemian Rhapsody', and its attendant uniqueness as an advertising vehicle, continued apace on the fitful journey northwards from Oval towards Soho, not least because the lyrics, now lodged firmly in my head once more, were impossible to banish. What other pop song lyric, I found myself wondering, possesses this kind of power? What other song lyric possesses the same sort of across-the-board impact? What other pop song possesses a similar kind of collective, cross-cultural, cross-generational resonance? Let's think ... 'Imagine' by John Lennon? Well, for a start, it would not have made me, or my partner, or countless other long suffering London Transport customers, break into an involuntary grin as soon as they clapped eyes on the lyrics, and then do the same again when they tried in vain not to inwardly sing them. Maybe, 'Like A Rolling Stone' by Bob Dylan? Again, no. Too specialized, too rarefied, and too intellectually challenging to fit the bill. How about Led Zeppelin's 'Stairway To Heaven', that other great epic but cryptic seventies' anthem, which, for a while, like 'Bohemian Rhapsody', threatened to be a millstone around its creators' neck? Again, it fails to pass muster. Too little known outside the heavy metal fraternity, too narrow a catchment audience. 'My Way', then, by Frank Sinatra? Nope. Too slow and old fashioned, and way off the mark in terms of the required tone.

I went on like this, racking my brain for a pop anthem that could have worked on me, on the general public at large, and on the predatory mind of the advertising copywriter in such a perfect way. I mentally trawled the Beatles' back catalogue, of course, and The Stones' greatest hits, and good old Elton's endless stream of hummable, sing-along-able pop tunes. I even turned to the relatively small, but recently inescapable, track records of upstarts like Oasis and, ever more desperate, The Spice Girls. But no, there was simply no substitute. It *had* to be, could only be 'Bohemian Rhapsody', a song that everyone with even a passing interest in popular music knows, but that no-one – bar possibly, but not definitely, the late, great Freddie Mercury himself – could possibly profess to understand.

Now, think about that for a minute. A song enters the collective popular consciousness on a global level while simultaneously staying resolutely beyond our individual logical, or even instinctive, understanding of its lyrics. There is a particular sort of genius at work here. A fiendish imagination. A Machiavellian pop mind. Now, consider that the song in question manages to merge the structures and shadings of light opera with the primal dynamics of heavy rock *and* the multi-tracked, baroque geometry of prog-rock. On top of this already rich cocktail, the singer, in mock operatic tones reminiscent in places of a Gilbert & Sullivan hero, delivers his unique narrative – if, that is, you could call the inspired lunacy of those lyrics, a narrative.

Farrokh Bulsara, 1947.

If the song's form recalls a Gilbert & Sullivan operetta – had that esteemed duo dabbled in psychoactive drugs – the content is closer to the associative word play and wilfully nonsensical verse of an older generation of English literary eccentrics like Edward Lear or Lewis Carroll. Then, just to gild the lily even more, the opus in question clocks in at nearly 6 minutes (5 minutes, 52 seconds to be precise, edited down from an original 7 minutes), when the unwritten rule of pop songwriting, stretching back to Chuck Berry, states that the average length of the perfect pop single is, as we all know, under three minutes. Having broken this cardinal, and usually dependable rule, and most of the other unwritten rules of pop as well, the record then shoots to the top of the pop charts like the proverbial bullet, and stays there, inviolate, unbudgeable, for 9 weeks; the longest spell at the top since Paul Anka's 'Diana' back in 1957. 'Bohemian Rhapsody', then and now, represents, among other things, the triumph of the implausible. It happened though, it really happened, and we have one way or another been living with the implausibility of its success ever since that fateful day, 29 November 1975, when it hit the number one slot.

Since then successive generations of, it must be said, often reluctant music fans have had their individual and collective consciousness colonised by those "scaramouches" and "fandangos", have hummed them, sung them, mocked them, tried to banish them, and, in the end, simply surrendered to them. (This, of course, is what that inspired copywriter behind the Tube ad campaign instinctively understood.) Since then, too, it has been voted Britain's best single of all time in the Music of the Millennium poll. It has become, courtesy of its inclusion in the American hit comedy, *Wayne's World*, a post-modern, post-slacker anthem. (What a trajectory!) And, though the group and their fans would be loath to admit it, it has also served as a no doubt unconscious template for an equally ambitious, equally inflated, equally long, but utterly un-tongue-in-cheek, contemporary prog-rock anthem, Radiohead's 'Paranoid Android'. (Whisper it softly, for they are precious and sensitive souls, not given to the kind of humour that underpinned many of Freddie's big and bold projects.)

In short, the legacy of 'Bohemian Rhapsody' has been as surprising, and indeed as implausible, as its original ambition. Of one thing, though, we are certain: there is simply nothing else like it in pop's endlessly self-referential, effortlessly self-perpetuating history. It is utterly unique. Singular. Unmatched. Just like its creator. So it is that, when we come to praise the late, great Freddie Mercury, even as we are doing now, in his much less feted solo capacity, it is, as I have just neatly illustrated, the

place we have to start from. In short, 'Bohemian Rhapsody' encapsulates everything that was inspired/inflated/insanely ambitious about Freddie Mercury, pop's most elusive, and, yes, most *mercurial* showman (His adopted name, like everything else about him, from his stage personae through to his costumes and his song titles, was carefully chosen.) It was the pivotal point where Queen moved from a popular post-glam, post prog-pop group to a pop phenomenon, and a pop phenomenon which, from that moment on – and this is hugely important, and often overlooked – defied all the defining critical and/or cultural shifts in taste and fashion of the previous thirty odd years. Until 'Bohemian Rhapsody', Queen were simply another rock group, albeit one who possessed a unified vision, and an attendant attention to detail that was rare in rock music. After 'Bohemian Rhapsody', Queen, and Freddie Mercury in particular, became something else entirely; something huge and unstoppable, something phenomenal.

Though both Dylan's 'Subterranean Homesick Blues' and The Beatles' 'Strawberry Fields' predated it, 'Bohemian Rhapsody' was also the first *modern* pop promotional video. Unlike its illustrious predecessors, it was widely seen and subsequently talked about almost as much as the song itself. It was also, then, and how could we forget, the moment where Freddie Mercury, in all his sparkle and splendour, his over-the-top otherness, his sheer, unavoidable *presence,* entered our pop consciousness with a fanfare that few entertainers, before or since, have matched. We didn't just listen to Freddie singing those mad lyrics, we saw him act them out in what we would soon find out was his own inimitable manner. There he was perched at the piano stool like a glammed up, singer-songwriter, then, briefly, in silhouette like Olivier as Richard III, then strutting through clouds of dry ice like the leader of a glam-metal stadium band, and – the *pièce de resistance* – prismed and repeated like a kaleidoscopic representation of himself. Talk about a statement of intent! Here, in the space of one albeit epic song, was Freddie the showman, the chameleon, the fantasist, writ large. Little did we know back then that this was just a mere hint of what was to follow.

MERCURY RISING...

We must delve some way at least into the childhood of Farrokh Bulsara, to try to extricate the essence of Freddie Mercury, the pop chameleon. He was born on September 5, 1946, to parents Bomi and Jer Bulsara, on Zanzibar, which the tourist brochures tell us is the island of exotic spices. (I often thought he should have reemployed the name Farrokh briefly for his dynamic creative pairing with Montserrat Caballé; it should have been his operatic name; and a neat line in semantic reversal – King Faroukh as opposed to Queen('s) Freddie.) His parents hailed from Gujarat in western India, and were of the Parsee faith, and thus followers of the man-god, Zarathustra.

Though born in Zanzibar, Freddie Mercury, né Farrokh Bulsara was emphatically Indian: he was educated at St Peter's boarding school near Bombay for ten years, and did not arrive in England until he was 17. Though he played down his ethnic origins, he should be remembered, and celebrated as, among other things Britain's first and biggest Indian pop star. (The Parsees, intriguingly, still see themselves as Persian rather than Indian, though they fled Persia over 1,000 years ago. Freddie's family, too, though born British-Indian, consider themselves a part of the Parsee race, a distinction that highlights the subtle but often deeply felt difference between citizenship and roots.)

It was in India that the seeds of Freddie's showmanship were sown. In the early photographs included in this book, you can see him making an impression as a sportsman – Best All Rounder and medal winner, and as a performer – acting in a school play, at St Peter's Boarding School, India, looking hammy but holding centre stage. Slightly older, he poses, dead centre, in a line up of the all-Indian combo, The Hectics, his first group, in which he played piano and sang tentative vocals on Buddy Holly and Elvis Presley songs. Older still, he lounges on a summer seat in the school grounds in 1962, looking like some self-styled Gatsby-type hero, in shades, crisp white shirt, pressed pants and matching shoes. It is preceding photograph, taken six years and a whole continent later, that is the most intriguing, though. Beneath a dandyish velvet hat, the hair has grown and is no longer brushed back. In jeans, t-shirt and bare feet, he nestles a Fender Stratocaster guitar in a distinctly Jimi Hendrix-style pose. He looks very different, altered, on his way to somewhere else, somewhere far from St Peter's Boarding School and the Hectics; far, too, from this spartanly furnished living room in Feltham, not far from Heathrow, Britain's gateway to the world.

The Bulsara family moved to England in 1964, fleeing the revolution that brought independence from British rule. As an adolescent pitched from one culture into another, Freddie seems, revealingly, to have had little trouble adapting to his new life. He went to Ealing College of Art in 1966, following in the footsteps of Pete Townshend of The Who and Ron Wood, guitarist with the Faces and later The Rolling Stones, and graduating with a Diploma in Graphic Art & Design in 1969.

In those three years, while Freddie studied art, the pop world shifted off its axis, and, from a rented flat in trendy Kensington, Freddie Bulsara dipped tentatively into London's burgeoning psychedelic counter culture. He shopped in Biba, swinging London's hippest emporium, and at Kensington Market, dressing in silks and velvets in homage to his hero, Jimi Hendrix. He later manned a stall there, alongside his new friend, Roger Taylor, selling Edwardian silk scarves, fur coats, exotic fabrics, alongside the graduate art work of Freddie and his more interesting fellow students from Ealing Art College. "We even sold Freddie's thesis," Taylor told *Mojo* magazine, "which was all based on Hendrix. There were some beautiful things – there was a Planetscape and he'd written the lyrics of 'Third Stone from the Sun'…" Freddie, who alongside Taylor, was now also a fully fledged member of Queen, confessed to having seen Hendrix "play live on nine consecutive nights – one show after the other." One imagines, given all that was to follow, that it was the image of Hendrix as much as the man's explosive music that held him rapt.

At his peak, Jimi Hendrix's onstage persona, as even a cursory glance at any remaining film footage shows, was mesmerising to the point of shamanistic. He dealt in the realm of extremes and paradoxes: androgynous yet intensely sexual; fragile yet explosively violent; a wraith in feminine silk scarves and velvet crotch hugging pants who would, on occasion, set fire to, then graphically act out a grinding, thrusting sexual assault on his guitar. It is well nigh impossible now to overstate the importance of Hendrix on British pop audiences, nor the catalytic impact he had on the legion of performers who flocked to his shows. Brian Jones and John Lennon, the doomed avatars of psychedelic pop, were constant presences stage front, as was the young, as yet directionless fledgling rock singer, Freddie Mercury.

ONE VISION...

It was five years on from that Hendrix-style photograph that Freddie Mercury – Freddie the chameleon, Freddie the already full-scale fantasist – first entered my life. Back then, as a young, uncertain teenager in Northern Ireland, sure only of one thing, that life was elsewhere, I was in thrall, not to pop music, but to rock music. Back then, there was a big difference. Pop music was Sweet and Mud and David Cassidy. Rock Music was the mighty Led Zeppelin and Roxy Music and David Bowie. Pop was singles; rock was albums. Pop was Jimmy Saville on *Top of the Pops*, which I still watched religiously because Bowie or Roxy, but never the mighty Zepp, might be on; rock was "Whispering" Bob Harris and *The Old Grey Whistle Test*, in which Bowie and Roxy and a whole host of even more exotic groups appeared with an at times alarming regularity.

Every Tuesday evening, if my memory serves me well, I would run across the road to a neighbour's to watch *The Old Grey Whistle Test* on BBC2, a relatively new channel. What I remember most vividly about those Tuesday nights in front of the television is how seriously "Whispering" Bob took his role as the keeper of the "real rock" flame; how, like a slightly stoned academic, he would reel off band family trees, album histories, remembered live gigs, in a hushed, reverent whisper as if imparting secret, sacred knowledge. Which, in a way, he was. What I also remember are the strange cartoons used to illustrate certain, usually brand new, tracks – this was the era before video killed the animator. I later found out that those cartoons were eagerly watched by stoned rock fans the length and breadth of Britain, a secret society of giggling *Whistle Test* aficionados, in thrall to

"I'm trying to say that classy people can be whores as well."

"Whispering" Bob's Zen cryptic ruminations and these weird, abstract animations as much as to the music. One week, it must have been in 1973, the track accompanying the animation was by an unknown group called Queen. It was called, we were gravely informed by "Whispering" Bob, 'Keep Yourself Alive'. As its title suggested, it was fast to the point of frantic, yet it possessed a certain sleekness, a sense that it had been worked on, sculpted, streamlined and polished. It was, we can now see, a statement of intent as much as anything.

The next I heard of Queen was a song called 'Seven Seas of Rhye', from the 1974 album *Queen II*. I was confused. I can see, in retrospect, why. Put simply, it sounded like a different group. Here is Cliff Jones, some time rock scribe and leader of a contemporary glam-pop group called Gay Dad, of whose name, at least, I'm sure Freddie would approve: "The lyrics hark back to Freddie's obsession with Tolkien." He wrote in *Mojo* magazine in August 1999, when Queen were featured on the cover, "Play this against anything from *Never Mind The Bollocks* (by The Sex Pistols) and it stands up. Although Freddie was wearing black jump suits with diamond studded gloves, this was essentially a punk track, a high-octane speed delivery and all the teenage aggression a great record needs. Forget people who say Queen are pomp-rockers – they blow the arse of any me-too punk band."

At the time, though, if truth be told, the four members of Queen – Freddie, drummer Roger Taylor, guitarist Brian May and bass player John Deacon – weren't certain what they wanted to be, and seemed to be touching all the bases from pomp to proto-punk in an effort to find out what they did best, where they fitted in. Later, of course, they would find out that, like all great pop bands, they did not fit in at all. That dawning realization must have occurred around the time of the next single, 'Killer Queen', which I would humbly suggest, was the first fully fledged Queen record proper: that is, a single that possessed a definite and, with hindsight, immediately identifiable signature. 'Killer Queen', a mini magnum opus, if such a thing can be said to exist, was more even sculpted and sleek than its predecessors, and less frenetic. It was also much more ambitious. Freddie claims to have written the lyrics "in a night", but, perhaps because of the song's quite complex lyrical and musical structure, the latter fitting the former like a glove, it sounds painstakingly crafted. The first thing that grabbed my attention were the lyrics, the tone of which is best summed up by the opening quartet:

"She keeps Möet et Chandon
In her pretty cabinet
'Let them eat cake' she says
Just like Marie Antoinette..."

Not, then, the regular subject of a rock and roll record, though both Mick Jagger and Bryan Ferry were, in their very different ways, indulging in what might be called posh-rock lyricism at roughly the same time. I have always assumed that 'Killer Queen' was about a high class transvestite – the monarch of the title being a drag rather than a regal queen. Instead, it was, as Freddie would later admit, somewhat reluctantly, "about a high class call girl," adding, no doubt self-mockingly, "I'm trying to say that classy people can be whores as well." Once the lyrical sophistication had sunk in, there was Freddie's high-camp, mock-operatic delivery – part Gilbert & Sullivan, part male diva – to absorb; intimations of what was to come. Then, in and around the words, were woven the multi-tracked vocal harmonies, and Brian May's harmonic guitar stylings, which would, from this moment on, remain a constant, defining feature of all Queen's subsequent great records. With 'Killer Queen', the group had arrived at a sound that was all their own. A sound that was not quite prog-rock, though it possessed identifiable traces of that inflated genre, not least the last vestiges of Freddie's Tolkein obsession; and not quite glam-rock, though it dallied near the same subject matter and dressed itself up in the same sequins and spangles. Back then, Freddie mostly wore satin and silk, his fingernails varnished blood red or jet black. He looked exotic, even slightly menacing at times, stalking the stage like he had to claim it territorially, make it his own.

I must confess here and now that I did not grow up with Queen as a soundtrack to my teenage years. Their music was not an integral part of my adolescent life in the way that certain Led Zeppelin or Roxy Music songs were. Nor did I rush out and buy their singles and albums on the day of release the way I did with the latter two groups. No, Queen's songs were simply there: on the radio, at the disco, in the background at parties. I kind of liked them, but, truth be told, my taste was for a rawer, more primal rock sound. I had, through the *NME*, discovered some even more exotic, slightly diseased specimens like The New York Dolls and Iggy & the Stooges, denizens of the Big Apple's musical *demimonde*. I was, without knowing it, waiting for Punk to happen. It happened, on cue, in 1976.

So, too, in a whole other pop universe, did Queen. Punk came and went in the twinkling of an eye, its fallout affecting all new music which came after it; Queen, defiantly a pre-punk group in their aptitude *and* their attitude, stayed the distance, resolutely defying the Punk purges and every other change in music and pop culture that followed after. (Queen are a footnote in Punk history, though. It was their sudden withdrawal from the *Today* television show, hosted by Bill Grundy, that led to The Sex Pistols appearing on the same, and gatecrashing the public consciousness in true Punk fashion with their swear words and generally obnoxious behaviour.)

The point where Queen began their journey into the pop stratosphere, and into our collective pop consciousness, was, as I have already illustrated, 'Bohemian Rhapsody'. After that, nothing was the same again. Looking back, it was, in its way, as momentous a single as 'Anarchy In The UK' by The Sex Pistols insofar as it represents a defining pop cultural moment from which there was no turning back. You were either on Queen's side from hereon in, seat belt fastened for the whole, big, bumpy ride, or you were bailing out of the emergency exit heading for an uncertain landing on planet Punk. I, dear reader, was of the latter persuasion. From 'Bohemian Rhapsody' in 1975 until the video for 'I Want To Break Free' in 1984, when I suddenly realised how mad, bad and subversive Freddie Mercury could be, I tried to live my pop life in avoidance of Queen and their music. I actively defined myself against everything I thought they stood for. And, of course, they simply grew bigger and bigger, more unavoidable, more inescapable.

Basically, Queen conquered the world, but they never conquered the pop press. That was their lot in the pop cultural scheme of things: always popular, never fashionable. "We were never critically acclaimed," Roger Taylor mused in *Mojo*, "which seemed to become quite important after a while because the more critically acclaimed you were, the more you were assured of failure." From the start, failure was not a word that featured much in the Queen vocabulary. "We aimed for the top slot and were not going to be satisfied with anything less," Freddie would recall years later. "We wanted the best. It wasn't a question of world domination, although I know it probably came across that way. You have to have a lot of arrogance and confidence, and an absolute determination … Arrogance is a very good thing to have when you are starting out in this business. That means saying to yourself that you're going to be number one, not number two, hope for the best and head for the top." Nor did they give a second thought to fitting in. It is worth remembering that Queen came up through the seventies, out of, but never really part of the key pop cultural contexts of that odd time. They began life when prog-rock and glam-rock were the predominant forms, but fitted in neither camp. They hit big in the mid-to-late seventies, when Punk was railing against all things big and bombastic, when the kind of music they played – epic, inflated, wide screen – was supposed to wither up and die.

And they continued to grow and mutate into a stadium rock roller coaster of excess and epic ambition throughout the early to mid-eighties, ignoring, or blithely aware of, their continuing unfashionability. While serious rock students nodded to the jangly guitar and bedsit solipsism of the Smiths and their imitators, Queen strutted and preened, loud and proud and unapologetic, on a different planet. In short, Queen were the rock group that ruled the world utterly on their own terms. Their 1975 album, *A Night At The Opera,* stayed in or around the top of the British charts for a year, reaching No. 4 in America. At the height of Punk, the follow up, *A Day At The Races,* topped the UK chart like a giant raspberry blown at Johnny Rotten & Co. So it continued: 1977's double A sided single, 'We Are The Champions' / 'We Will Rock You', said it all and, as was their wont, said it loud and clear and in-your-face. Likewise, the anthemic 'Radio Ga Ga', complete with a video that, unconsciously or otherwise, drew parallels with stadium rock grandiosity and Third Reich rallies. They became tax exiles. They released a single called 'Fat Bottomed Girls' / 'Bicycle Race', accompanied by a video that left little of the song's

innuendo unexplored. They became the rock group the pop press and the Left *really* loved to hate when they played eight shows in Botswana's Sun City – a rare wrong move in the area of public relations – and were subsequently placed on the United Nations' cultural blacklist. Impervious to accusations of, in no particular order, bombast, blatant sexism and political irresponsibility, they just kept on keeping on.

In the music press, tales of Queen's – and Freddie's – eighties' appetite for excess were legion. We were never invited to their album launches or after-show parties – he hated the music press, and the *NME*, where I then worked, in particular, ever since an article about him was published under the headline, Is This Man A Prat? – but we heard all the stories. We heard about topless – and even bottomless – waitresses serving champagne, about lesbian double acts laid on to entertain the inner circle, about transvestites, drag queens and dwarves with shaved heads on which were arranged long lines of Colombia's finest cocaine. (The latter story has entered the realms of legendary rock and roll anecdotes, up there with the Stones' and Led Zeppelin's oft-reported debaucheries, though denied by all and sundry.) As their one-time stylist, Diana Mosley attests, "Queen could certainly throw a party." In 1978, they celebrated the release of the *Jazz* album with an all-night bacchanal in New Orleans, featuring the cream of the city's strippers and transvestites, and all manner of weirdness that included sexual contortionists and a guy who cavorted under a pile of chopped liver! "It was deliberately excessive," recalled Brian May years afterwards, "partly for our own enjoyment, partly for friends to enjoy … partly …" (and one feels he is being truthful here) "… for the hell of it."

And, still, Queen grew and mutated, commercially conquering all before them. Rock in Rio in 1985, Live Aid later the same year and Knebworth in 1986 became the three live shows that illustrated their extraordinary, and unassailable, position as the biggest performing act of the eighties. The first virtually drew a whole city to a standstill; the second saw them literally conquer the world, via a seamless seventeen minute medley of hits that stole the global thunder from under the noses of the cream of the world's pop elite; the third was their last live show, a spectacular homecoming before an audience of a quarter of a million on a – wait for it – six thousand square foot stage.

Sometimes, along the way, though, Queen did occasionally stumble and fall. Pre Live Aid, on albums like 1978's *Jazz* and 1982's *Hot Space,* they seemed lost, like a group going through the motions. During recording of *The Game,* in Munich in 1980, they fought bitterly, over direction, even over royalties. "We all tried to leave the band more than once," Brian May admitted later. "Then we'd come back to the idea that the band was greater than any of us. It was," he added almost ruefully, "more enduring than most of our marriages!" Basically, the motivation that had sustained them for so long had dissipated. They had, in short, achieved most of what they set out to do, and felt jaded, lacking in incentive. They had grown blasé about their success, their bigness. Live Aid, though changed all that. "They were absolutely the best band of the day," organiser, Bob Geldof enthused, "They played the best, had the best sound, used their time to the full. They understood the idea exactly – that it was a global juke box. They just went and smashed one hit after another. It was the perfect stage for Freddie: the whole world."

And, on that day in July, 1985, Freddie Mercury was indeed the main man, the centre piece, the great entertainer. Even stripped of his props, his lavish stage designs, his extravagant costumes, Freddie Mercury shone

brighter than the rest. (It was his performance at Live Aid, too, that led to his official selection as one of the Post Office's millennium icons, alongside Charlie Chaplin. Freddie Mercury's image duly appeared on a stamp, designed by pop artist, Peter Blake, the man responsible for the most famous album cover of all time, The Beatles' *Sergeant Pepper's Lonely Hearts Club Band*. "I had never been to a Queen concert apart from Live Aid," elaborates Blake, "but I could feel the enormous rapport between the group and the audience, and that's what I wanted to capture. The top half of the stamp is taken from those giant screen images that feature in big events, and the bottom is an expression of the same moment in the live performance. It was that multi-faceted element I wanted to capture. I was trying to capture the spirit of Live Aid which, I believe, reignited Queen's career." Incidentally, Roger Taylor, who is just visible behind Freddie, and behind the drums, is the first living Englishman, other than royalty, to be featured on a stamp.)

I WANT TO BREAK FREE…

Back there, then, for a long pop moment, Queen were *it*. The biggest, the most bravura, the most knowingly, wilfully garish; the rock group as pure spectacle, pure entertainment. And yet, there was subversion in there too. Sometimes it was unconscious – the bass line from 'Another One Bites The Dust' travelled way beyond the group's control, sampled to such a degree that it now is regarded as one of the key musical motifs that kick-started a whole genre, hip-hop. 'We Are The Champions' coupled with 'We Will Rock You', too, travelled lunar distances from their intended meanings: 'We Are The Champions' becoming one of the most enduring football terrace chants as well as a stadium rock anthem; 'We Will Rock You' being similarly adopted by American baseball and ice hockey fanatics.

And sometimes the subversion was a whole more obvious, but no less powerful. Where his sexuality was concerned, Freddie walked a tightrope between complete discretion and outright exhibitionism, never openly declaring that he was gay but coming out so obviously – so totally in his videos, his personas, and his projected self – that only the deaf, dumb and blind, or the totally deluded, could fail to guess his orientation. The sudden appearance of the moustache, the gay clone look, the post-Village People macho man image, all said, "Look at me! I'm gay!" He may as well have worn a big sign, featuring those words written in day-glo colours, around his neck.

"Freddie *lived* gay," his erstwhile stylist, Diana Mosley elaborates, "he didn't have to shout about it, or even come out. He had that flamboyancy that was gay, but he didn't see himself as a figurehead. He didn't want to be public." Still, it appears that many of his fans thought otherwise. Or simply didn't think about it at all. Miranda Sawyer, writer and pop journalist for *The Face* and *The Observer* speaks for many when she says, "I grew up listening to Queen, seeing this outrageous character on video, and I never once thought that he might be gay. He was simply larger than life in the way that real stars were meant to be. I just thought he was an outrageous performer, given to dressing up. That's the power of pop fandom, it can blind you to the obvious."

The apogee of Freddie's outrageousness, at least on the public stage, remains the video for 'I Want To Break Free', a song from their thirteenth hit album, *The Works,* released in 1984. This was the moment when I, a snobbish rock critic who had dismissed Queen as simply a showbiz irrelevancy, big but meaningless, began to think twice about the band I had done my best to ignore ever since 'Bohemian Rhapsody' had colonized my pop consciousness back in 1975. Began to think twice, to be exact, about this character called Freddie Mercury.

'I Want To Break Free' was made at a time when the pop video form had become, in certain instances, more important than the music it was meant to promote. The cost, too, had spiralled accordingly, with the likes of Duran Duran and Michael Jackson making their promo-videos for budgets that could have funded small feature films. Queen's, of course, were not impervious to this kind of extravagance; in fact they positively thrived on it. Their previous single, 'Radio Ga Ga', a Roger Taylor composition that mocked the increasing blandness of pop radio, had employed 500 extras, dressed in silver boiler suits, to clap in time to the chorus. It had been their most expensive video to date, and it had worked; the single hit the number one position in 19 countries across the globe. Given all this, and the fact that the group were now huge in Middle America, an important market that had proved stubbornly resistant to various British invasions since the heyday of Led Zeppelin's all conquering cock-rock, 'I Want To Break Free' was a brave move. Some might say, a suicidal one. Written, like 'Another One Bites The Dust', by John Deacon, the song was tailor-made for Freddie, who obviously saw it as another moment to come leaping out of the closet once more on video, though this time in the most blatant way imaginable – even by his outrageous standards.

The first image is of a hairy, bangled arm pushing an old, fifties' Hoover. Then, a be-wigged Freddie emerges, clad in a pink sleeveless top that strains to cover the most outrageous pair of falsies, a vinyl micro-mini skirt, stockings, suspenders and stilettos. He hoovers around John Deacon, nestling in drag on a sofa, reading the *Daily Mirror,* looking for all the world like that weird old lady that Terry Jones used to play in all those cross-dressing Monty Python sketches. In a suburban living room, filled to the brim with period kitsch, including three china ducks flying in formation, Freddie hoovers and pouts and sings about how (s)he wants to break free. Around him, Roger Taylor poses by the cooker every inch the sexy schoolgirl, and Brian May scurries past to root in the fridge, resplendent in a pink night gown. I can still recall the first time I saw the video: the initial shock – what the hell is going on here, exactly? – turning to delight, then to admiration at the sheer cheek and the sheer hilarity of it all. A hilarity Freddie revels in – that collusive wink to the camera as he starts singing the opening lines, then that regal toss of the head as he banishes a stray lock of hair from in front of his eyes. Priceless.

Then, when you think it simply cannot get any more outrageously camp, Freddie pushes the living room door open to reveal a whole other planet of camp. The suburban house gives way to a set that would not look out of place in the English National Opera, as Freddie, in black and white body suit pays homage to Nijinsky in Debussy's *L'Apres-Midi d'un Faune.* He blows on a horn, rolls across the prone, outstretched bodies of

Freddie and Mary Austin backstage during Queen's 1974 UK tour.

the extras, and leaps off a rock into their adoring arms. Mad! Hilarious! Knowingly, brilliantly, totally camp. Pure Freddie Mercury.

But in the living rooms of Middle America this was a leap too far into irony and campness; two concepts that remain relatively alien to the transatlantic blue collar rock audience. "I remember being there when the video for 'I Want To Break Free' came out," recalled Brian May years later, "and there was universal hatred and shock and horror. It was, 'they dressed up as women! How could they do it?' It was not a rock and roll thing to do and it wasn't something that was accepted – cross dressing in videos if you please! It was a really big shock. I think the midwest of America suddenly perceived that Freddie might actually be gay. That was shocking. That was not allowed. It was a bit scary…"

Though this reaction seems scarcely credible now, it was, alas, too true. On the back of that brilliant, groundbreaking, and hilarious video, Queen more or less lost their mass America audience. "The thing about Queen," elaborates the American rock producer, Arthur Baker, who has worked with New Order, Ash and a host of other British groups, "is that they always confounded their audience's expectations. Perhaps too much so for heartlands America. When I was growing up in Boston in the seventies, they were the hip hard rock band you had to like. They even displaced Led Zeppelin for a while. Nobody, though, got that Freddie was gay and that there was a whole other level of meaning going on in his songs. Even the name, Queen, didn't give it away. It simply never crossed people's minds. Or else, they fooled everybody. To this day, I'm not sure which. All I know is that they kept me on my toes; I had them pegged as a hard rock group, then 'Another One Bites The Dust' became the most played record on R&B stations – a huge black radio hit. Then I saw the video for 'I Want To Break Free' and, boy! I mean, I was on the floor! It was the funniest, most over-the-top pop video ever, but outside New York and maybe the West Coast, Americans just didn't get it. It offended the rock audience which in America, is essentially a very conservative audience. Cross-dressing? A gay rock singer? I mean, forget it!" Whatever, as Baker acknowledges, there is nothing quite like it in contemporary pop. Probably because no one else would have the imagination, the humour, the vision, the sheer, bloody minded nerve.

I WANT IT ALL…

The term mercurial is defined in my *Oxford English Dictionary* as 'sprightly, ready-witted and volatile'. It would not be overstating the case to suggest that Freddie Mercury, the man as well as the pop chameleon, lived up to his adopted surname, and then some. He lived a complex life, one characterized by seeming contradictions. Though he was Britain's first Indian pop star, he was secretive to the point of paranoid about his roots in Zanzibar and India – his first publicist never even knew his real name. Looking at Farrokh Bulsara in some of those early teenage photographs, it is not difficult to see where his insecurity, and his attendant longing to be accepted, to be loved – which Freudian psychoanalysts would say is the key determinant, rather than ambition, of the will to succeed – stemmed from. He looks, even dressed up like a Gatsby hero and lounging on a

summer seat, gauche and slightly ill at ease with himself. His prominent teeth, which earned him the nick name 'Bucky' at St Peter's School, were a lifelong source of unease, but he feared that cosmetically altering them might affect the timbre of his singing voice.

In a world where England and America provided the predominant physical role models for the rock and roll look, from Presley onwards, his otherness, ethnic and cultural, must initially have seemed like a burden, and perhaps one he never totally transcended. Of such a deep-rooted sense of otherness, though, is the star born. And because it is an arena which encourages, which celebrates otherness, because it is a place where the outsider can find not just a home, but a huge empathetic audience, the pop life is nearly always a complex, contradictory one. In all of his contradictions, then, in his almost total self-belief *and* his attendant insecurity, Freddie Mercury was not unique. And yet his life, particularly after his initial success, was a uniquely complex one. His first important, and enduring, romantic relationship was with a woman, Mary Austin. They lived together as boyfriend and girlfriend, albeit he the attention-seeking extrovert, and her the quiet, reflective introvert. It is difficult to imagine a more diametrically opposed significant other for Freddie than Mary Austin. And yet … and yet, their friendship, their love endured.

Mary met Freddie before he was famous, when Queen were still in the embryonic stage, meeting and rehearsing, trying to fit together the beginnings of a sound. Initially, she saw him as "a kaleidoscope personality," someone "who opened my eyes to a lot of colour … he would see the irony in life, he looked for the humour. He did not like the darker side." Later, as his fame increased, and his once suppressed sexuality blossomed, their love affair, in Freddie's own words, "ended in tears." To both their credits, they remained close, as close as it is possible to be between a man and woman without a physical element in the relationship. "A deep bond grew out of it (our love affair) and nobody can take that away from us. It's unreachable." he once admitted, adding, as if we hadn't got the message, "All my lovers asked me why they couldn't replace Mary, but it's simply impossible."

This is complex stuff. A gay man, who would confess to having "had more lovers than Liz Taylor," holds on to a profoundly heterosexual ideal of enduring romantic love. Perhaps, in love, as in life, Freddie simply wanted it all, and, in Mary Austin, he came as close as he could to the romantic ideal of perfect coupledom which, despite his bouts of promiscuity, obviously attracted him. Writing about him in *The Sunday Times* in November 1996, to mark a photographic exhibition of Freddie's life at the Albert Hall in London, the broadcaster and cultural commentator, Waldemar Januszczak, noted that: "Although he was outrageously camp in private, Freddie had always been coy in public about his sexuality. No, not coy: misleading. He certainly kept it hidden from his parents. In all the photos I see of the many Bulsara gatherings he attended, he is accompanied by Mary Austin, the former boutique owner whom he dearly loved, with whom he once lived, and to whom he left the bulk of his estate. Jim Hutton, the live-in lover who nursed Freddie through the worst years of his illness, is nowhere to be seen."

Freddie and Montserrat Caballé.

After he had broken up, at least physically, with Mary Austin, and his success grew, he surrounded himself with a retinue of real friends and admirers, as well as would-be suitors and hangers-on. It became known as the court of King – though surely that should have been Queen – Freddie. He threw extravagant parties in Munich, New York and, most notably, in Garden Lodge, his London home. For a while, both off-stage as well as on, he was the epicentre of attention, a living, breathing, larger-than-life illustration of the term, party animal. It inevitably took its toll, emotionally as well as physically. "My affairs never seemed to last," he once noted, ruefully, "There must be a destructive element in me, because I try very hard to build up relationships, but somehow I drive people away … Love is Russian roulette for me. No one loves the real me, they're all in love with my fame and my stardom."

Love is Russian roulette for me. Boy! For a while back there, though, as he admitted more than once, Freddie literally played Russian roulette in the wilder gay clubs of New York and Munich, rather than London where he was simply too well known not to attract the attention of well meaning fans and the not so well meaning paparazzi. As far back as the second Queen tour of America in 1976, he told tabloid journalist Rick Sky, that "Excess is part of my nature. To me, dullness is a disease. I really need danger and excitement … I am definitely a sexual person … I love to surround myself with strange and interesting people because they make me feel more alive. Extremely straight people bore me stiff. I love freaky people around me."

To this end, he delved deep into a subterranean world where casual sex was not so much an option as a given. In his sexual life, he was, as with almost everything else, a risk taker. But, as we now know, in the eighties, the stakes were high; the gamble was literally a life and death one. "He went where angels feared to tread," Rick Sky told Freddie's biographer, Lesley-Ann Jones, "he was that classic refined person who loved to slum it. His ultimate fantasy would be to take a rent boy to the opera." Instead, in 1987, having settled down somewhat in London, following a wild, hedonistic period living in Munich, he took himself to the opera and brought home a diva. It was the last, and most unlikely, of all the great projects that Freddie Mercury undertook in his relatively short, totally incident-packed lifetime.

A NIGHT AT THE OPERA

"The opera queen must choose one diva. The other divas may be admired, enjoyed, even loved. But only one diva can reign in the opera queen's heart, only one diva can have the power to describe a listener's life, as a compass describes a circle."

Wayne Koestenbaum: *The Queen's Throat – Opera, Homosexuality and the Mystery of Desire* (Penguin Books)

"We went to Zandra and said we want some stuff which is going to reinforce our dramatic potential. She was very into it, she's a very dramatic lady. It was very uncool to do this kind of stuff – people in those days almost without exception went on stage with very little lights so you couldn't see them anyway and wore jeans and T-shirts."
Brian May.

"Freddie was very pumped up about that Zandra outfit and how much he loved it. He loved what the arms did, the fact that they gave him wings. I remember when I shot him that day he wore his winged shoes with it."
Mick Rock, photographer, photo taken Summer 1974.

The opera queen in question was Freddie Mercury; the diva, Montserrat Caballé. It would be poetic to say they found each other, but, in reality, Freddie found her. She, until then, was blissfully unaware of his existence. In his extraordinary book, *The Queen's Throat* – how Freddie would have loved that title! – Wayne Koestenbaum unwittingly points to part of the appeal of opera to someone raised in, and on, rock music, which, even at its most vaultingly ambitious, its most bombastic, its most, in fact Queenly, does not come close to the ambition and bombast of *Aida* or *Carmen*. "The volume, height, depth, lushness and excess of operatic utterance," he writes, "reveal, by contrast, how small your gestures have been, how impoverished your physicality..."

Which is probably why one of the few, if not the only person, to render Freddie Mercury speechless, dumbstruck, was today's diva incarnate, Montserrat Caballé. He discovered her in May 1983 during a production of Verdi's *Un Ballo In Maschera* (A Masked Ball), which he had attended, with his assistant, Peter "Phoebe" Freestone, primarily to see and hear the world's most famous living tenor, Luciano Pavarotti. "Pavarotti came on and sang an aria in the first act, and Freddie thought it was brilliant," elaborated Freestone in Lesley-Ann Jones' biography of Freddie, entitled simply *Freddie Mercury.* "In the second act the prima donna came on, and it was Montserrat Caballé … She started to sing and that was it. Freddie's jaw dropped. He only wanted her from then on…"

The album they eventually recorded together is, to me, the musical centrepiece, the one utterly realized triumph, of the triumvirate of solo albums gathered in this lavish package. It is a record in which Freddie's voice comes alive in a way that it does not on any of his other solo works. The impatience with the constrictions of rock and pop that showed itself from time to time throughout his career – initially in his stretching the boundaries of the form with 'Bohemian Rhapsody', itself a mini rock-opera in three parts – now finds a release in the company of a *proper* singer. (The first thing he said, revealingly, when he heard her almost ghostly tone, was, "Now, that's a real singer.")

What I love about the coming-together of Freddie Mercury and Montserrat Caballé is, in a way, the same thing I love about 'Bohemian Rhapsody', and the video for 'I Want To Break Free' – the ambition, the nerve, the devil-may-care attitude of the man. There is something implausible about the idea of a pop singer and an opera singer duetting, something that suggests a no-win situation, a stand-off or a compromise between low and high culture, in which neither will emerge victorious. Or dignified. This, however, was not the case. Freddie understood Montserrat, and she understood Freddie; they revelled, from the start, in each other's company, staying up until the early hours, singing show tunes and pop tunes and light opera tunes around the piano. They were divas together, in consort, in harmony.

Inevitably, they found a stage big enough for both of them, performing in Barcelona with the city's Opera House Orchestra and Choir before an audience that included the King and Queen of Spain. The occasion was the La Nit open air festival, during which the city formally received the Olympic flag from Seoul. (That they actually mimed, rather than sang – due to Freddie's recurring problem with throat nodules, the singer's nightmare – hardly mattered, it was the sense of occasion, of symbolism that was important.)

In many ways, the Montserrat Caballé duets on the *Barcelona* album represented Freddie Mercury's last great triumph. Sure, there was another solo album and more Queen hits after it, but this collaboration was more than anything else, a triumph of the will. He saw a chance to reinvent himself outside rock music, and he made the leap. And what a leap, of faith, of confidence, of self-belief. Listening now to the other solo work collected here, it is possible to get a glimpse of yet another Freddie Mercury, someone both confident in his singular abilities, yet strangely adrift without the other 'three' around him. There is emotion and musical range aplenty on both *Mr Bad Guy,* which, in commercial terms, was not a success, and *The Great Pretender* (the US version of *The Freddie Mercury Album,* and an altogether more fitting title), and they add to the received image of Freddie Mercury, entertainer, chameleon, dropping in and out of musical guises with consummate ease. They suggest to me a man trying to reach out, but not entirely stretching, his abilities: it's almost as if he was tentatively testing the waters for a future solo career. Who knows?

Personally, the Freddie Mercury of *Barcelona* is a more exciting, not to mention intriguing, prospect. You can literally hear how excited he is, how inspired and excited by the newness of it all, by the challenge. He is, in short, in his creative element. It, alone, is worth the price of admission; it is also a fitting valediction to a life lived against the grain, against expectations, against constraints, both creative and social.

THE SHOW MUST GO ON…

"Those were very sad days, really, but Freddie didn't get depressed. He was resigned to the fact that he was going to die. He accepted it; we were all going to die someday. And, anyway, could you imagine an old Freddie Mercury?"

Peter Freestone, quoted in *Freddie Mercury* by Lesley-Ann Jones.

Freddie Mercury was officially diagnosed HIV positive in 1987, one year before the *Barcelona* album. His final years were spent in London and Montreux, among a close circle of friends that included his personal assistants Peter Freestone and Joe Fanelli, his manager Jim Beach, and the second great love of his life, Jim Hutton. "He took on board and accepted the inevitability," Mary Austin remembers "I saw a man become incredibly brave." He told each of his immediate circle in turn, plus the band, all of whom had expected the worst for some time, instructing each of them not to speak of the matter again. "He accepted," says Peter "Phoebe" Freestone, "that he was one of the unlucky ones. He had no regrets. Well, maybe one – that he had so much music left in him." To this end, he recorded with Queen for as long as he could. When the other band members officially found about his illness they "clustered around him like a protective shell," as Brian May memorably put it. Queen made a further two critically acclaimed albums, *The Miracle* in 1989, and *Innuendo* in 1991, the singer, to the end, insisting on what were now physically exacting standards of quality control.

In his second last video appearance, dolled up like a deranged Lord Byron, Freddie sang 'I'm Going Slightly Mad'. The man had style, and attitude to burn. In the last Queen video, 'Days of Our Lives', he looks fragile, ethereal, as if he could be borne away on the wind at any moment. Gone are the extravagant gestures, the constant movement, replaced

"Those were very sad days, really, but Freddie didn't get depressed. He was resigned to the fact that he was going to die. He accepted it."

by a fragile, still dignity. His last words on film were, "I still love you," whispered intimately to his adoring public. A diva until the end.

One of the last characteristically extravagant things Freddie Mercury did was buy an apartment in Montreux, near Queen's recording studio, and decorate it in grand style, knowing that he would never live there. A final act of defiance against encroaching mortality. Likewise, his insistence that he should dine out to the end, often spending days in bed so that he could have the energy to entertain his friends at an exclusive restaurant. Pure style, pure class. Amid the picture postcard serenity of Montreux, which he once would have found boring in the extreme, he seemed to find a sense of peace and solitude, the very things he had spent much of his life running from. He spent days looking out on the lake, lost in private reveries. He wrote two final sad songs, 'A Winter's Tale' – the title said it all – and, with Brian May, the elliptically biographical 'Mother Love', a song about returning to the womb. A song about safety, comfort, spiritual, emotional and physical solace.

Back in London, he began to paint and draw for the first time since leaving Ealing College of Art. Propped up on his in bed, he drew his cats, painted abstract watercolours. Queen's fortieth single was released in October 1991, entitled 'The Show Must Go On'. Pure bravado, pure Freddie, pure Queen. The b-side was 'Keep Yourself Alive'. On 23 November, a statement approved by Freddie was issued to the press confirming what many had suspected, that Freddie Mercury had AIDS. He died the following day. A statement was issued at midnight: "Freddie Mercury died peacefully this evening at his home in Kensington, London," it stated, simply, "His death was a result of bronchial pneumonia, brought on by AIDS."

At his cremation, the music was a recording of 'You've Got A Friend' sung by Aretha Franklin. As the oak coffin disappeared into the flames, the recorded voice of Montserrat Caballé sang *D'Amor sull'ali rosee,* the aria from Verdi's *Il Trovatore*, Freddie Mercury's all time favourite piece of music. Even in death, he had a talent to surprise.

Made In Heaven, a Queen album that employed digital technology to bring all four members of Queen together again, even in Freddie's absence, was a fitting epitaph, though ironically, it was, in tone and content, the least Queenly album the group ever released – stately and reflective, heartfelt and tender. Finally, the many masks that had hidden the true face of Freddie Mercury seemed to have slipped during

the writing and recording of these last valedictory songs. "My make-up may be fading but my smile stays on," he sang gamely, but there was an honesty, a vulnerability on display here that was touching, and touchingly unfamiliar.

On 20 April, 1992, the other three members of Queen hosted a Freddie Mercury tribute concert at Wembley Stadium, featuring an array of guest vocalists singing what amounted to Queen's greatest hits live. George Michael, David Bowie, Annie Lennox, Liza Minnelli, Axl Rose and, of course, his great friend Elton John were among the stellar line-up, with Elizabeth Taylor, tireless AIDS campaigner and celluloid diva incarnate, making a speech in Freddie's honour. His absence though, was keenly felt on that Wembley stage, as artist after artist gave full vent to those anthems and love songs and epics; every performance, ironically, calling to mind the master. Where Queen's back catalogue of hits is concerned, nobody, but nobody, does it better that Freddie Mercury. The Mercury Phoenix Trust was also established that year, and continues to raise money for AIDS related causes. In 1991, 'Bohemian Rhapsody' was re-released, and once again, went straight to number one, raising over a million pounds for the Terence Higgins' Trust.

No one knows where Freddie Mercury's ashes are scattered bar those that were closest to him. There is no monument to Freddie Mercury in Britain, save his musical back catalogue. On his birthday, and on the anniversary of his death, fans congregate at Garden Lodge, where Mary Austin now lives, surrounded by Freddie's cultured legacy – the fine art, the artefacts, the Empire furniture, all the expensive and aesthetically pleasing fragments he shored up against his final departing. Every year, Mary reads them a short statement, a prayer of remembrance. I am reminded, even in the nature of his death and the mourning that still attends it, not of a mere pop star, but of Valentino, of Callas. Freddie, I'm sure, would approve of the comparisons.

He would surely approve too, of the eight foot-tall statue of him in full-on performance mode that has, since 1996, looked out from a plinth on the Montreux shore line across Lake Geneva, sculpted by Irena Sedlecka, a Czech monumentalist best known for the heroic reliefs that decorate the entrance to the Lenin museum. Fist raised, biceps taut, Freddie stands in stadium rock pose, facing the sunset across the lake, his back to the curious and the faithful who flock to the site. "If I had known he would have his back to the people," Irena remarked afterwards, "I would have spent more time on his bum."

"I think Queen songs are pure escapism, like going to see a good film."

THE GREAT PRETENDER

Where, ultimately, do we place a performer as singular, as chameleon-like as Freddie Mercury? He was certainly a pop star (and, for a while, way back there, lest we forget, a rock star); he was also an entertainer par excellence, as well as a scene stealer, a risk taker, and a diva. But he was also much bigger and much more complex than all of those labels.

In an era when rock music often became literally strung out on its own importance, weighted down with all that attendant angst and anxiety, Freddie Mercury created a public image, and a series of personas, that harked back to an older time when entertainment and escapism went hand in glove; when the very essence of entertainment was the providing of escapism. "I think Queen songs are pure escapism," he said, "like going to see a good film. After that, they (the audience) can go away and say, 'That was great!' and go back to their problems."

There is a great, and enduringly relevant Hollywood film called *Sullivan's Travels*, written and directed by Preston Sturges in 1941. Its hero is a hugely successful Hollywood studio director, the Sullivan of the title, whose string of big production romantic comedies have all been box office smashes. Gripped by the desire to do something meaningful, something both truly artistic and socially worthy, he sets off to travel depression era America, disguised as a tramp, in order to research a social conscience movie about the lot of the common man. After a series of adventures, including wrongful imprisonment, he realises that what the common man wants is not social messages or political education but … you guessed it … entertainment, escapism.

Freddie Mercury never had to make that journey of discovery: every fibre of his being, every impulse that drove him to be bigger, brighter, brasher than the rest, told him that pure, unadulterated entertainment – the triumph of the spectacle, of the illusion – was a worthy and exalted end in itself. Because of his dedication to rock music as entertainment, and, by extension, his dedication to entertainment as escapism, we – particularly us critics – thought we knew Freddie inside out. We thought we had him in a nut shell. We saw him, as indeed he sometimes saw himself, as The Great Pretender, trying on guises, personas and images like ordinary mortals try on clothes. Because he was, as he told us over and over, simply a "natural performer", an "extrovert", we do not accord him an iota of the pop cultural import we heaped on far less successful, but more "serious" performers. (Interestingly, the late Kurt Cobain, the leader of American band Nirvana, and the last great figurehead of angst-ridden rock and roll, wrote in his suicide note that he felt he was short-changing his fans and could never ever be a great entertainer "like Freddie Mercury". While both Beck and Sonic Youth, two stalwarts of American independent rock, have name checked *Queen II* as an influential album.)

Because he wilfully ignored the baggage of rock and roll – the angst, the anxiety, the suffering for your art – we filed him away in a corner called, simply and pejoratively, "entertainment for the masses". (As if, given what we know about the century's great entertainers, from Chaplin to Minnelli, there was anything simple about that all-consuming calling.) Which, on one level, is all probably just as well because Freddie, even from the little that we – his public, the critics – know of him, would have been the last person to want that kind of cultural canonization. His last instructions to Jim Beach, his manager, were "Do what you like but never make me boring!"

And yet we know that he was hurt by the put-downs and the critical pastings, which reached a nadir of sorts with the now infamous mid-seventies' *NME* feature entitled Is This Man A Prat? "I'm a very hated person…" he confessed, "I think I've learnt to live with it. I'd be a liar to say I'm not hurt by criticism, because everybody is." We know, too, that he had his revenge, the ultimate revenge, in fact, on the self-appointed taste-makers, on the hipper-than-thou critics, on the pop cultural snobs; put simply, the more they ignored him, the bigger he grew. And the bigger he grew, the more impossible-to-ignore he became.

As with all relatively short, but incredibly rich lives, it is difficult to know exactly where to begin in attempting to place Freddie Mercury in the greater scheme of things. In pop cultural terms, he was nowhere near as influential nor as enigmatic as pop's more serious icons – the likes of Dylan, Lennon, Hendrix or Prince – and it would be wrong to judge him critically against them. That, as I have already said, was not where he was coming from.

He did not want to try and change the world through his words and music like Dylan or Lennon, nor even change the course of pop music like Hendrix or Prince; he simply wanted to sparkle and dazzle, snag our attention, *all of it,* for a brief moment, then move on. This intention, however throwaway, is, of course, the essence of great pop, and maybe even – though the jury is still out – of great rock. Thus, even when Freddie Mercury was being over-vaultingly ambitious – and what was 'Bohemian Rhapsody' if not an exercise in vaulting ambition, always close to, but never quite teetering into total absurdity? – there was in his work an attention to detail but not necessarily to depth. "There are no hidden messages in our songs…" he insisted, more than once, as if the very idea was anathema to his essentially showbiz sensibility. Freddie, in musical terms at least, was pure surface. But boy, what a surface. What a dazzling, sparkling, kaleidoscopic surface. What a showman. What an illusionist. What a chameleon. Right to the end.

Like Madonna or Elton John or even Maria Callas, Freddie Mercury ultimately became, through the sheer size and ubiquity of his celebrity, one of those stars whose fame ultimately transcends their work. That is, he entered the popular pantheon to become a celebrity who was no longer primarily famous for what he did – write, record and perform songs – but simply for who he was – Freddie Mercury, mega-star. That, of course, has always, to an extent, been the self-serving, self-perpetuating nature of fame: eventually you are famous simply for being famous.

These days, though, we live in an age where celebrity has colonized the public consciousness like never before; where the minutiae of famous, and increasingly semi-famous lives, relayed in detail through a voracious media, exercise our imagination to an at times unsettling degree. The endless passing parade of second and third division *faux* stars whose dull gaze, repeated *ad infinitum* from the pages of the tabloids and lifestyle mags, reflects our own jaded interest, and has debased the value, the currency of celebrity. We have become, in the process, almost inured to the appeal of the *real* star, the *true* star. *Almost.* Freddie Mercury, I contend, was a true star.

Sometimes we didn't see it, particularly we critics who increasingly look for meaning beyond the obvious, but it was there all along, staring us in the face. Freddie Mercury had star quality, charisma, presence – call it what you will – in spades. For a start, he had an intuitive understanding of the contract between celebrity and his adoring public that was old-style, almost vintage Hollywood, in its application. He was, for instance, both offstage and on, more Liza Minnelli than Mick Jagger. He was showbiz *and* he was rock and roll, but ultimately, he was a lot more showbiz than rock and roll. (I'm talking old school showbiz here – Garland, Astaire, even Valentino, to whom Freddie, only half-jokingly, often compared himself – "I'm a true romantic, just like Rudolph Valentino.")

He had an old-school professionalism and, from day one, a precocious grasp of the contract that even rock and roll demanded: "These days, music and talent is not enough. You have to be able to do more than write a good song. You have to deliver it, and package it… You must learn to push yourself, and learn how to deal with the business side right from the start… Go out there and grab it, utilize it, and make it work for you… You have to feed it to the masses… It's called Hard Sell."

Had he been around during the first golden age of Hollywood, or the dawning of the rock and roll era, or had he blossomed during the psychedelic sixties, you get the feeling Freddie Mercury would have applied himself to the task in hand with ambition, wit and style, would have made it big. That's simply the way he was; he thought, acted, lived BIG. He knew, too, how to maintain a sense of mystery and a sense of privacy. He knew how much to give his fans and how much to hold back for himself and his intimate circle. He was an inveterate party thrower, and a present giver, showering his true friends and intimates with well chosen, often extravagant gifts at every opportunity. He lived life to the full in the manner of a true diva.

With hindsight, then, it is possible to place Freddie Mercury in a lineage, or a tradition, that is even more outside pop and rock and roll than we might like to think. His penchant for mock opera – 'Bohemian Rhapsody' of course, and a dozen or so other songs which, though not as *outré,* betray a certain impatience with the constrictions of mere rock and roll – is one clue to the myriad forces that shaped him. Likewise, his late flowering love of *real* opera and ballet, both of which betray a mind in thrall to aestheticism and exotica, to older, more colourful,

and – this is perhaps revealing – more demanding entertainments than the rock performance.

You can also, without delving too deep, detect traces of music hall and old style variety in some of Freddie Mercury's lyrics and in his delivery of them, particularly during his more camp moments, both live and on record. In his costumes and stage presence, his myriad personas, and, most of all, in that strutting, preening, posturing commitment to all things over-the-top, he recalls too, the older magic of nights at the circus, the carnival, and, of course, the opera. (Remember that tight fitting body suited decorated with huge false eyes? Pure circus surrealism.)

Which is to say that there was always, right from the start when he was tarted up in satin, chiffon and black nail varnish, something exotic, something other worldly about Freddie Mercury. Those Zandra Rhodes costumes, for God's sake. I mean, what other rock group, save maybe the Stones in the early seventies, or the misunderstood, much under-rated New York Dolls, would have gone to such lengths to look so wilfully effeminate so early in their career? (Interestingly, Freddie's image became less other-worldly, less *outré,* as he accepted and embraced his sexuality, his costumes pared down to almost caricatured expressions of gayness – the moustached macho man, the leather clone, the drag queen, the body narcissist in tight black hot-pants and *Flash* t-shirt. But there was always the self-deprecating humour; the leather clone outfit was spot-on save for the ballet slippers and socks. It was as if he had to poke fun at himself, at his own sartorial outrageousness before someone else did. What, I ask you, would Freud have made of that?)

On the occasion of the Freddie Mercury Photographic Exhibition, the posthumous celebration of his life which opened at the Albert Hall in London (since then it has toured the world visiting many cities including Bombay, Cologne, Montreux, Timisoara and Paris – no half measures even in death) Waldemar Januszczak wrote "Transplanting levels of fantasy that belong in *1001 Arabian Nights* – that was Freddie's achievement." For a self-styled simple entertainer, that was no mean feat. He was ultimately, I believe a weaver of spells, a creator of personas, masks, mythologies, a fantasist. "A lot of my songs are fantasy. Really, they are just little fairy stories. I can dream up all sorts of things because that's the world I live in." He was, we can see with hindsight, someone who literally willed his fantasies, on-stage and off, to come through – and, perhaps more crucially, to come true.

To this end, his life was lived in the glare of the spotlight and the flash gun, but neither stole his soul, nor, as the events of his final years proved, compromised his dignity. He remained a showman, an illusionist, and a chameleon right to the end; both a diva who played to the gallery right up to his final curtain call, and an intensely private individual who, even in death, did it his way.

Some, but by no means not all, of his achievements in life have been recognized posthumously by the fact that he has topped polls for being both a unique rock singer and an inspirational hero for the Asian community.

As elusive and mercurial as his adopted name, Freddie Mercury was a one-off, and the pop world is a less glamorous, less outrageous place without him. Of one thing we can be certain: we will not see his like again. And, while his larger-than-life statue dominates not just a Swiss lakeside but also theatres where Queen's sell-out musical *We Will Rock You* is playing, we will quite rightly find it impossible to forget him.

Freddie Mercury

A LIFE IN PICTURES

The earliest picture of Freddie, aged six months, taken on the East African island of Zanzibar where he was born Farrokh Bulsara on September 5, 1946. This was taken by a local photographer, who won a prize with this picture and proudly displayed it in his shop window, so perhaps this counts as Freddie's first public appearance.

"It was an upheaval of an upbringing, but one which seems to have worked for me."

Proud mother Jer shows off the seven month old Farrokh in the garden of the family home in Zanzibar. Happy times for the family while Freddie's father Bomi worked as a cashier in the Zanzibar High Court, the young Farrokh always seemed to be smiling, as can be seen here. Freddie's mother Jer recalls that as a baby Freddie loved to pose for the camera.

Nanny Sabina, who would look after the young Freddie until he reached the age of four, spending the day with Freddie and putting him to bed at night. It was one of the privileges of growing up in Zanzibar and his father Bomi's position that the family would become accustomed to having servants, something his mother Jer would have to make him aware he would have to do without later in life if he succeeded in persuading the family to move to England.

Freddie, 8 or 9, with Kashmira, his younger sister, on holiday in their grandparents' home town of Bulsar in the Gujerat province of western India. It was from the town name that Freddie's family – like many others from the region took the family name. The Bulsara's took a lengthy holiday in Bulsar every four years when his father Bomi would be entitled to a six month leave of absence from his position at the Zanzibar High Court.

Freddie on his 4th birthday in Zanzibar, wearing his prayer cap and birthday celebration garland traditionally worn for Temple blessings on special occasions such as birthdays and weddings.

On his way to the Fire Temple for his 4th birthday blessing. The family might otherwise have travelled by local taxi, but mother Jer wanted her son to experience the more traditional rickshaw ride.

Freddie would leave Zanzibar to attend boarding school at St Peter's in Panchgani, India at the age of seven. The school was private and English, and it was here that he began to be called Freddie. He turned out to be a star pupil, winning this cup for 'Best Achiever'. Mother Jer recalls, "He was an all-rounder, in studies and in sports. Whatever he turned his attention to, he succeeded in."

While at St Peter's Freddie won a number of medals for sports. This was the medal won on Sports Day for coming second in the high jump. Freddie also excelled at boxing, which his mother Jer tried to dissuade him from. "I didn't like him boxing. It was a very rough game."

Notice too, the phoenix on the medal. It seems that it was the St Peter's school emblem that inspired Freddie to design the Queen crest. The crest comprises the zodiacal signs of each band member, and, apparently, the phoenix head and wings from Freddie's old school motif.

35

The original Bicycle Race. Everyone at St Peter's had a bicycle. Freddie's mother Jer believes that it was these days at school that inspired Freddie to write the classic Queen song.

Spot the actor: drama was another interest for Freddie at
St Peter's. "He liked anything artistic," says mother Jer,
"and one day wanted to do drama, so he tried that as well.
Anything that gave him a chance to pose!"

That unmistakable smile again, Freddie, centre, lining
up with The Hectics, the quiff and slacks giving little
indication of the outrageous stage wear that was to become
his trademark in later performing years.

39

It is said that while he entered St Peter's unsure and vulnerable, it didn't take Freddie long to regain his confidence, as this picture of Freddie taken in 1962 near to the end of his time at St Peter's shows. Curiously, Freddie thereafter appeared to give up the sunglasses until 20 years later and the 'Crazy Little Thing Called Love' tour.

In addition to all his other pursuits at St Peter's, Freddie was also taking piano lessons, reaching Grade Four in practical and theory. These led him to start his first band, The Hectics, apparently named after his naturally exuberant playing, as seen in this shot of the beaming Freddie at the keyboard.

In 1963, with Zanzibar heading for independence from Britain, the Bulsara family decided to leave. It was Freddie who pressed for the family to move to England rather than return to India, despite mother Jer's cautions that there would be no servants, and the family would have to "work hard". Freddie won, and the Bulsaras moved to Feltham, Middlesex. Freddie posing as Jimi Hendrix with a borrowed Fender Telecaster, photographed in his bedroom by a friend in 1968.

In 1966, Freddie left Isleworth Polytechnic with an
A level in Art and enrolled at Ealing Art College to study
Graphic Illustration. A world apart from the regulations
of his previous boarding school, Freddie very quickly settled
into the more liberal atmosphere of his new college, the
St Peter's quiff and slacks giving way to a more casual
Freddie, as seen here snapped in a friend's back garden
during his graduation year, 1969. Later Freddie was to
say: "Art school teaches you to be more fashion conscious,
to be always one step ahead."

With contemporaries at Ealing Art College who included
Peter Townshend and Ron Wood, it is not surprising that
Freddie became intrigued by the possibilities of a career in
music. In his final year of college, he joined his first serious
band, Ibex. Freddie seen here relaxing with members of the
band in West Kensington, London.

With his band Ibex, Freddie played his first live performance at Queen's Park, Bolton on August 24, 1969, photographed here. It was during this period that he also changed his name to Mercury, originally thought of as naming himself after the messenger of the gods, a fact later corrected by his family, insisting that he chose the name because Mercury was his rising planet.

1972 was the breakthrough year for Queen. The band played five live dates around London which led to them being signed to the new EMI Records label and beginning work on their first album. This live shot capturing Freddie during those dates was later adapted to become the cover of that first album, Queen. Explains Brian May: "The artwork for our first album was coming on nicely – Freddie and I had been working on a collage of Doug's (Douglas Puddifoot) pictures for the back cover. But the front cover was still a problem. One night I was flicking through the photos and I suddenly realized what a striking image Freddie in the spotlight made.
I cut him out (cutting off his leg!), pasted him (slightly reduced) back on the spotlight image, and suddenly it jumped out as a cover. I remember thinking very consciously – 'Freddie as singer will be our figurehead – let's use him as such!'"

1970 saw Queen formed, but, curiously, it wasn't until three years later that they undertook their first photo session. This was staged at Freddie's flat in Holland Road, Kensington. Warming up for the thousands of sessions that were to follow, this is Freddie at that historic photoshoot.

"This is the man who performed 'I Want To Break Free' in drag … the man who sang 'Bohemian Rhapsody' upside-down with the Royal Ballet … the man who stole the show at Live Aid with the whole world watching."

On April 9, 1973 Queen returned to London's famous rock venue The Marquee, along with Imperial College one of their favourite London venues, for the third and last time. Now signed to EMI, the record company used the date to launch the band. Three months later the first album Queen *reached the Top Thirty and Queen moved up from clubs to play universities and city halls. No more dressing rooms like this one for Freddie!*

Brian May: "John Anthony (co-producer Queen *album – centre of photo) popped in after our very small gigs – he was a good morale booster because he always gave the impression that soon we would be signed up and on our way to public visibility – it took a long time. They should have preserved that grubby little 'dressing room' – actually a corridor to the toilet in the old Marquee in Wardour Street – what a piece of history…"*

(Note: Brian believes the figure to right is Mary Austin.)

Brian May: "My favourite shot of us together. I have
one on our studio wall. It was taken from underneath
the (only!) vocal monitor – this is the blurred black
shape at the bottom. Little did we know what the years
would bring…." Freddie wears his snake armband from
Kensington market. Brian is modelling an early Zandra
Rhodes outfit!

"We were unbelievably inexperienced but utterly confident
of our potential – I imagine we were pretty un-magnificent
that night – but the gig won us our first contract – a
publishing deal with Feldman Music. Freddie never
had any doubts, as you can see from this picture. He was
already the Great God Mercury!"

"Hope for the best and head for the top.
That's the only way to approach this business."

"It was just one of those flashes of inspiration that happen sometimes." Photographer Mick Rock was shooting Queen for the cover of Queen II early in 1974 when he showed Freddie a photograph of Marlene Dietrich taken by Hollywood photographer John Kobal. "This pose is culled from that Dietrich shot. There was a feeling that it might be pretentious. To Freddie that word was meaningless – 'but is it fabulous?' was all that mattered. Those were the days of androgyny, and Freddie was prepared to push it quite a way."

Left: Freddie photographed again in his favourite Biba jacket in 1974. "He wore it all the time, until he started to make some money and found Zandra Rhodes. You had to be very careful with his make-up; he was very conscious of his overbite and the way his chin would look. I remember asking why he didn't have his teeth done, he said he was afraid it would change his voice."
Mick Rock.

Above: "In those early days seeing Queen on stage I couldn't believe how big they projected themselves in such a little area. Freddie was no shrinking violet, he was pretty expressive. I hadn't seen that in anyone outside of Bowie and Iggy Pop. This was Freddie just before he discovered Zandra Rhodes!"
Mick Rock.

"There didn't need to be a reason to do a photo shoot. I was a camera fiend and Freddie was a great camera subject. We'd be hanging out together and Freddie would say "come over tomorrow and let's take some pictures." This was Freddie in his front room in Holland Road. The kimono came from a second hand store; Freddie didn't have any money at that time and became good at roaming around markets and second hand stores. Celia my make-up girl was holding a mirror to reflect the light coming in the window from Holland Road to create that zigzag of light which hits his eyes." A 1974 photo shoot with Mick Rock.

"When I shot this session with Queen when they first played the Rainbow in London in March 1974, no-one really knew who the hell they were – the first album hadn't really happened for them. Then Queen II came out, and by the time they came back to The Rainbow eight months later to end the UK tour they were massive. That album really changed everything."
Mick Rock.

*Above: Backstage at the Rainbow Theatre, London in
November 1974.*
*Left: At a photo shoot in Primrose Hill, London on
September 4, 1974.*

*Freddie photographed by Mick Rock on his bed at his flat
in Holland Road in 1974 in his favourite jacket of the
time from Biba across the road in Kensington. "Mary was
in the kitchen making tea and Freddie kept taking breaks
to listen to Joni Mitchell or to look at his Richard Dadd
books – which gave him the lyrics for his song 'The Fairy
Fellers Masterstroke' on* Queen II. *We were both a bit
loony and high camp and you can see that in some of the
pictures."*

*April 1975 saw Queen visit Japan for the first time to
play eight dates. It was the start of a lasting love affair for
Freddie – he became completely absorbed with the lifestyle
and culture. Japan was one of the first international
markets to open up in a major way for Queen and home
to a number of historic appearances by the band. Among
the band's most enthusiastic supporters was* Music Life
*magazine, which on this first visit presented them with a
best album of the year award.*

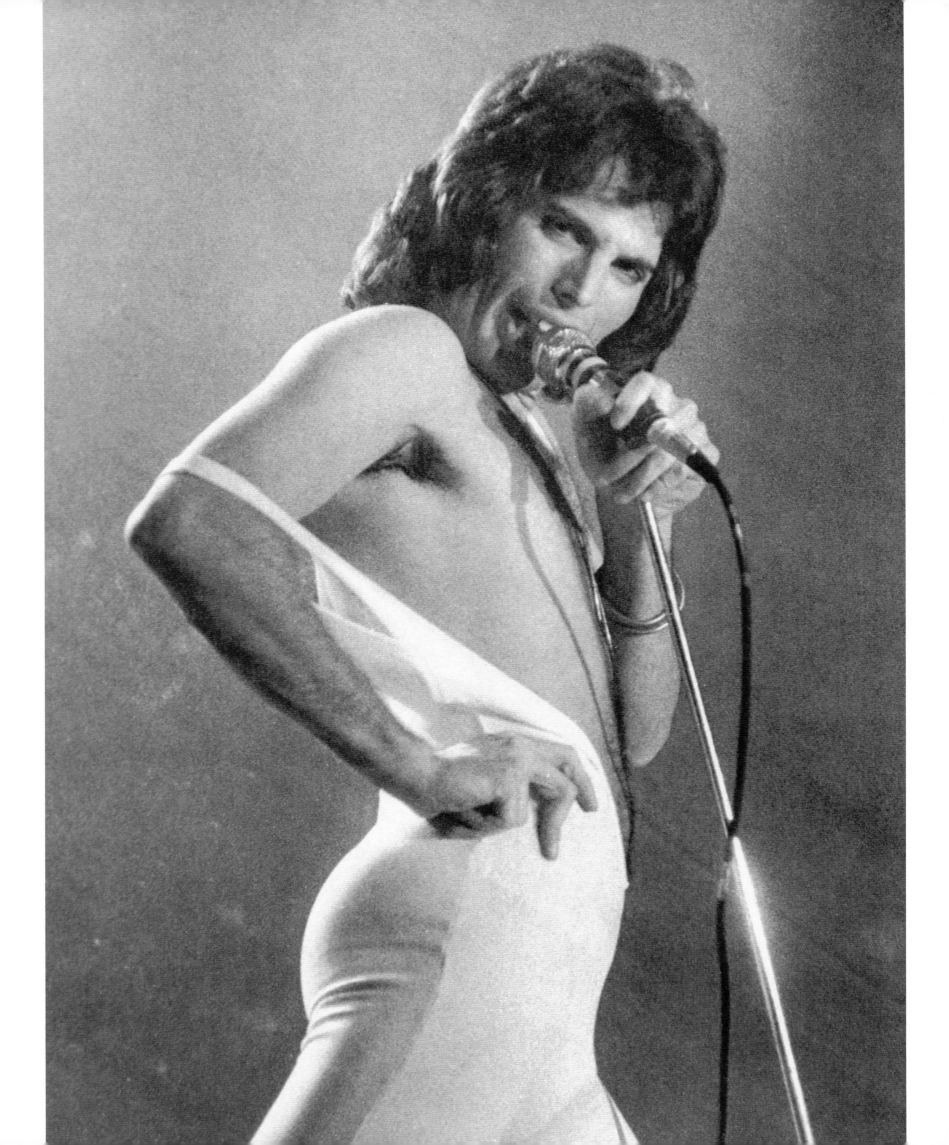

From Brian May's private collection, 'In the Lap of the
Gods' – "I have no recollection of who took this picture and
donated it to me, presumably I was busy at the time! This
is Freddie at his most 'glam'." Brian May. Freddie on stage
circa 1974, the year in which Freddie's stated ambition for
Queen to "be regal and majestic. We want to be glamorous,
and we want to be dandy," was beginning to crystalize.
The band had two top 10 albums, Queen II (April) and
Sheer Heart Attack (October) and for almost half the
year were on the road, touring Australia, the USA, the
UK (twice) and in the same period began their assault on
Europe with their first proper tour. Unfortunately the UK
leg had to be cut short when Brian took ill and collapsed
during the tour. Freddie was sanguine: "Sure a whole tour
would have helped us a bit more, but there's no such thing
as 'We lost our chance'. They were beautiful and they just
want us to come back as soon as possible."

"I think what Freddie brought (to Queen) was this
awareness of the bridge between the music and the public
and it was almost like a dirty word in those days, the
showmanship. He had an immense talent, an immense
depth of creative energy, so I think it was Freddie who
brought us to the point where we were ready to be seen.
'Killer Queen' era – this is Freddie with his real chest! The
newspapers, getting it completely wrong as usual, thought
that Freddie had worn a chest wig, the confusion arising
because Freddie had shaved his chest for one early photo
session! Here is the real thing …"
Brian May.

"There were a lot of things we needed to do on Queen II *and* Sheer Heart Attack *but there wasn't enough space. This time there is. Guitar-wise and on vocals we've done things we've never done before. To finish the album we will work till we are legless. I'll sing until my throat is like a vulture's crotch." Freddie talking at the time of recording of* A Night At The Opera, *photographed by Brian May during the sessions at Ridge Farm in 1975. "This is one of my favourite pictures of Freddie, in relaxed mode, in Biba T-shirt, creating at a frightening rate whilst we were writing and recording, putting this album together."*
Brian May.

*A kimono-clad Freddie taken early in 1975 during
Queen's first visit to Japan. After that visit in April,
Freddie announced: "I liked it there, the lifestyle, the art —
I'd go back there tomorrow if I could."*

A historic end of year for Freddie and Queen. Just two days before this picture was taken of Freddie at London's Hammersmith Odeon, December 1, 1975, 'Bohemian Rhapsody' had topped the charts for the first of nine weeks. Just over 3 weeks later A Night At The Opera *reached the No. 1 spot on the album chart. At the time Freddie defended himself and the band against their critics: "A lot of people slammed 'Bohemian Rhapsody', but who can you compare that to? Name one group that's done an operatic single. We were adamant that 'Bohemian Rhapsody' would be a hit in its entirety. We have been forced to make compromises, but cutting up a song will never be one of them!"*

Queen closed their massive UK winter 1975 tour with a special Christmas concert on Christmas Eve at London's Hammersmith Odeon, broadcast live across the country on BBC Television and Radio One for a special edition of BBC 2 television's The Old Grey Whistle Test. *Freddie was much amused by the idea that this was Queen's own special Christmas broadcast to the nation…*

Left: Live in the UK: A Night At The Opera tour, winter 1957.

Right and overleaf: 'Bohemian Rhapsody' changed everything for Queen. They were growing and mutating into a 'stadium rock roller coaster'. Outside of the UK their biggest arena for Freddie to preen and perform in was the USA. Peforming in ever increasing venue sizes, Freddie was in his element. The trail of excess that was to follow was taking seed – bigger, better, became the motto. "We're riding the crest of a wave", was how Freddie viewed the times, summed up in this shot (right) taken at Springfield Civic Center in February 1977 during the Queen Lizzy North American tour.

January 1977 – "Freddie had great fun with his new state-of-the-art Polaroid instant camera, snapping all his friends, and, with his usual generosity, giving away most of the photos to the sitters!
I snapped him in a snapping moment on stage during a sound check."
Brian May

"We owned the USA for a couple of years," Brian May recalls. 1977 saw two massive tours, the year sandwiched for Queen between the early Queen Lizzy tour and the News of the World *tour with which they ended the year. For Freddie these were heady days, America fully living up to its reputation as the land of plenty – so much so that Queen became tax exiles that year. For singer Annie Lennox this period in Freddie's career is a defining moment in rock history: "For me Freddie represents an era when people were less afraid of living life to the full. This was the seventies when rock's extravagances went beserk. There's a glorious rebelliousness about it, of freedom attached to it, that represents the whole spirit of rock 'n' roll."*

*Freddie in stereo – "I almost always carried a stereo camera
with us on tour, and there are many pictures of us on-stage
and off in this medium.
These pictures can be viewed by the 'magic eye' technique,
relaxing the eye so that the two images form one, but the
best way is to use a stereo viewer.
The result of course, is a 3D image, which is very lifelike."*
Brian May.

*Freddie's fashion transformation took seed during the
band's 1978 North American tour. Sequins and body suits
were being replaced by leather and PVC, Freddie's hair
several inches shorter.
"By the time I arrived in 1979," says Peter Freestone,
Freddie's personal assistant and dresser, "the Zandra
Rhodes originals were screwed up carelessly into crumpled
balls in the wardrobe trunks. The first clothes I had to buy
were three pairs of red PVC trousers, skate-boarding knee
pads and wrestling boots."*

North American Tour 1978.

"Freddie's look started to change during the Crazy Tour of Britain in late 1979 – although I still had to blow dry his hair during the guitar solos.
He picked up the look during the North American Tour. The moustache was to hide his teeth. Everyone in New York was wearing T-shirts and singlets so Freddie did the same. The leather shorts were originally trousers; Freddie cut them down."
Peter Freestone.

"I'd like to be carried on stage by six nubile slaves!"

Queen's 44-date US tour during the Summer and Autumn of 1980 ended with four concerts at New York's Madison Square Garden, the last on September 30. Earlier in the year Queen had topped the charts with 'Crazy Little Thing Called Love' and four days after leaving America, the band reached No. 1 again with 'Another One Bites The Dust'. Freddie was always happy to return to New York, so much so that for a while New York became his second home, when he bought a flat on 58th Street. In New York Freddie felt he could behave more like an 'ordinary person.'

"We are a very competitive group. We are four good writers and there are no passengers."

*"Freddie loved the attention he and the band got in
Argentina, especially from the local police – the band were
always surrounded by motorcades, and smuggled into and
out of gigs in armoured vehicles. All that attention became
a talking piece for Freddie, that would later always be
brought up in conversation.
It was, after all, history in the making."*
Peter Freestone.

*Having conquered virtually every other part of the globe,
Queen took on South America during 1981, becoming
the first major rock act to tour. Playing massive stadium
dates, Queen pioneered Argentina, Brazil, Venezuela and
Mexico. Over two nights at the Morumbi Stadium in Sao
Paolo, Brazil, the audience totalled over 250,000. "Never
had Freddie witnessed an audience on that scale," recalls
Peter Freestone,
"It took hours following the show for Freddie to
come down."*

The heavy security imposed by the Buenos Aires military
police during the band's stay had some advantages for
Freddie: "It meant that for once Freddie wasn't confined
to his hotel room. What Freddie loved most about the city
was that he was able to go shopping; even that far away
from home Freddie knew how to shop. He also spent a lot
of time being driven around the city seeing the architecture
and the gardens which he said reminded him of Paris.
They might have looked frightening, but mostly the
military police were in awe of the band."
Peter Freestone.

Freddie and the band preparing to go on-stage during
the South American tour, 1981. Freddie summed up his
feelings on the experience: "We came to South America
originally because we were invited down; they wanted four
wholesome lads to play nice music. Now I'd like to buy up
the entire continent and install myself as president."

Backstage on the South American tour, 1981, and an
unusual sight – Freddie strumming a guitar. "It was rare
to see that; Freddie wasn't fond of the guitar; he was only
able to play four chords and didn't like that."
Peter Freestone.

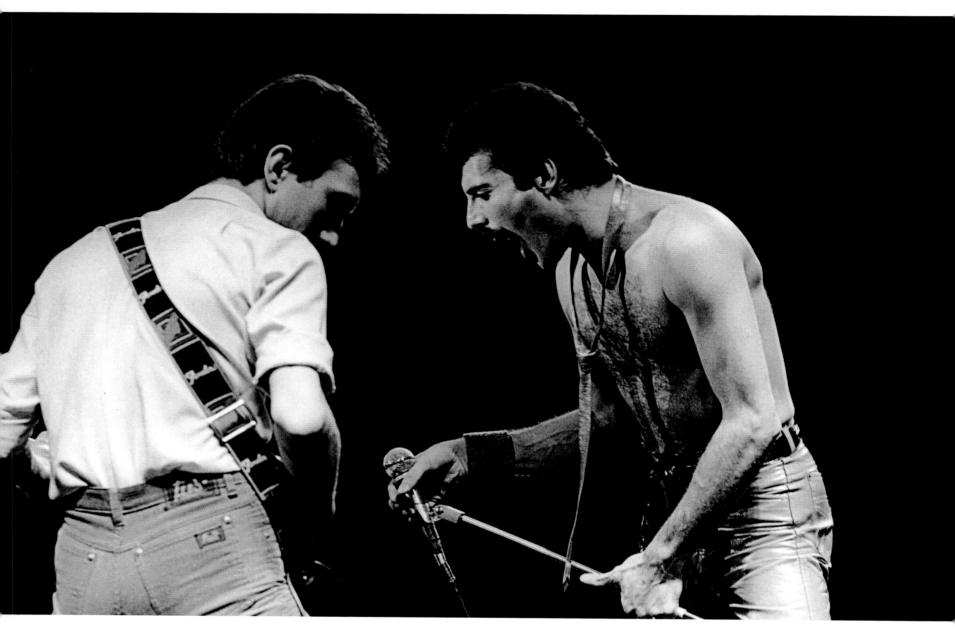

*Queen's South American tour ended with three shows
in Mexico in mid-October 1981. It had been a difficult
series of dates – national politics, the death of a President
(Betancourt), and the inexperience of many of the locals
involved had all added to the pressure – but Freddie and
the band retained their sense of humour – even though
the final night's audience in over-exuberance showered the
stage with batteries, rubble and even metal bolts, one of
which still remains in personal assistant Peter Freestone's
archive collection.*

Freddie and Roger backstage in Mexico, 1981

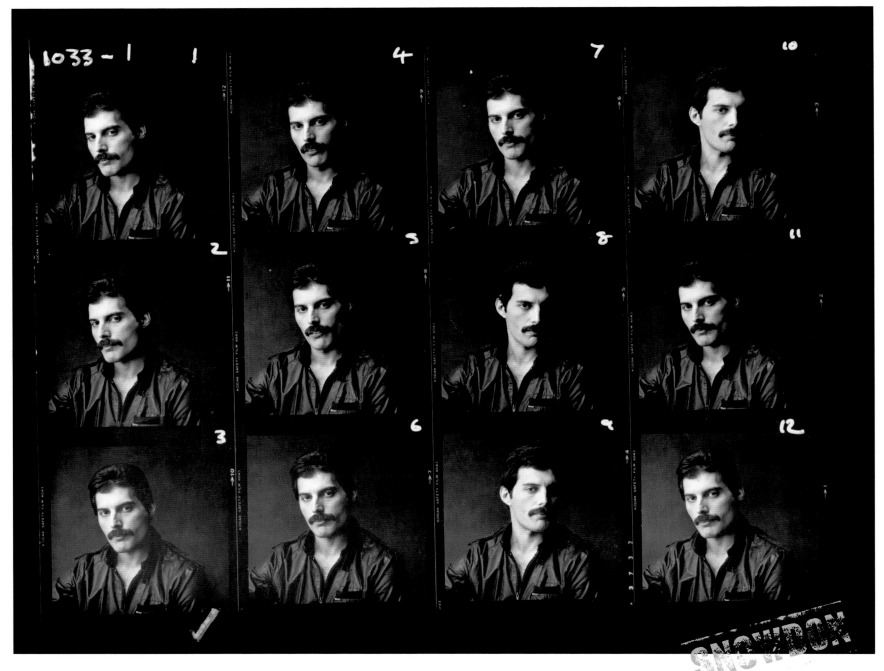

"Freddie loved working with known people, people famous for their work in some area, so sitting for Lord Snowdon for the Greatest Hits *cover in 1981 really appealed to him. I think he might also have been a little nervous, which is maybe why he looks so serious."*
Peter Freestone.

"The leotards got shifted out in 1979," says Peter
Freestone. "Freddie was spending a lot of time in North
America and became very influenced by leather. Freddie
had started wearing PVC with all sorts of holographic
pictures of American landmarks on them, now he was
adopting the uniform: leather jackets, T-shirts and the
biker cap." Freddie performs 'We Are The Champions' on
Queen's last North American tour, 1982.

Ironically, although the fashion of the 1980s had its roots
in gay culture, Freddie's new look appeared only to enhance
his machismo, especially across Middle America which had
previously had its doubts about the catsuits and leotards.

*Freddie with parents Jer and Bomi Bulsara on one of their visits to his Kensington flat in the early eighties.
It is unusual to see Freddie with both Jer and Bomi since for most family pictures Bomi would be behind the camera taking the shot.*

The Duck House on the edge of Lake Geneva in Montreux, Switzerland, became Freddie's haven from the attentions of the media during the latter part of his life. It was his home during the time that he recorded his last songs with Queen at Montreux's Mountain Studios and where he wrote his final song, 'A Winter's Tale', the lyrics immortalizing the breathtaking views across the waters of the lake he enjoyed each day and the sense of peace the retreat gave him.

"There are times when I wake up in the morning and think, My God, I wish I wasn't Freddie Mercury today."

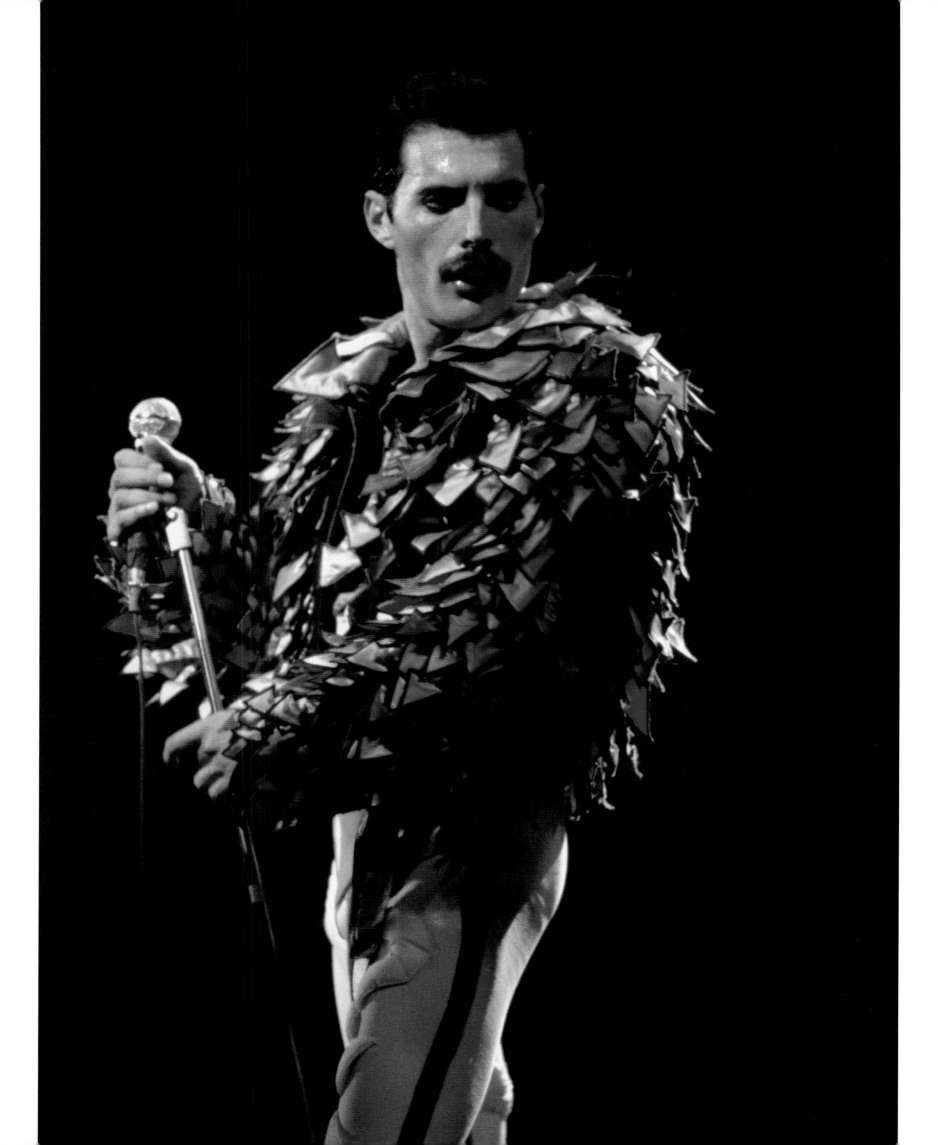

"I like leather. I rather fancy myself as a black panther."

Queen's 'Body Language' single of April 1982 gave rise to a whole collection of 'arrows' costumes which Freddie had had made for the 1982 Hot Space Tour.
This 'arrows' jacket was made up of hundreds of satin padded appliqué arrows hand stitched one by one onto the costume. "Freddie loved it, but it wasn't very practical," says Peter Freestone. "It was so heavy, and once on, it was so difficult to get off that it made a quick costume change impossible. In the end Freddie stopped wearing it."

Another 'Body Language' arrows jacket which Freddie had made in Los Angeles to wear on Queen's 1982 North American Hot Space tour. Freddie was so taken with the arrows look that he had several jackets made in different colours. This black and red leather one was a favourite.

Japan was one of Freddie's favourite places to tour and visit, especially for the shopping trips on which he would indulge his passion for lacquer boxes and other Japanese art. His appreciation of the culture and art of Japan stayed with him throughout his life. Freddie also made lasting friends in Japan, among them his music publisher, Misa Watanabe, seen here with him on Queen's 1982 Hot Space tour.

Hollywood photographer George Hurrell's work with the greatest screen stars, including Freddie's idol Marlene Dietrich, was much admired by Freddie. Freddie got to sit for the great man when he photographed Queen in his Los Angeles studio for the cover of the 1983 The Works album. "It was the first time I had seen Freddie not in total control and pleased to be so. I saw a very different Freddie that day, rather like a child sitting for a family portrait. Freddie was on his best behaviour."
Peter Freestone.

Among Freddie's closest friends was Elton John, or 'Sharon', as Freddie affectionately referred to him [if you were part of the inner circle you were destined to be granted a new title by Freddie: hence assistant Peter Freestone became 'Phoebe', roadie Peter Hince 'Rattie', manager Jim Beach 'Sylvia la Plage', names by which many remain known today]. Conflicting touring schedules meant Freddie and Elton were seldom in the same place at the same time, but on one rare occasion they got to appear on stage together – at Manchester's Apollo Theatre during Elton's UK tour in late 1982. Not wanting to be outshone on stage by Elton's baubles and braids, Freddie cunningly borrowed one of Elton's military styled outfits before joining him at the piano.

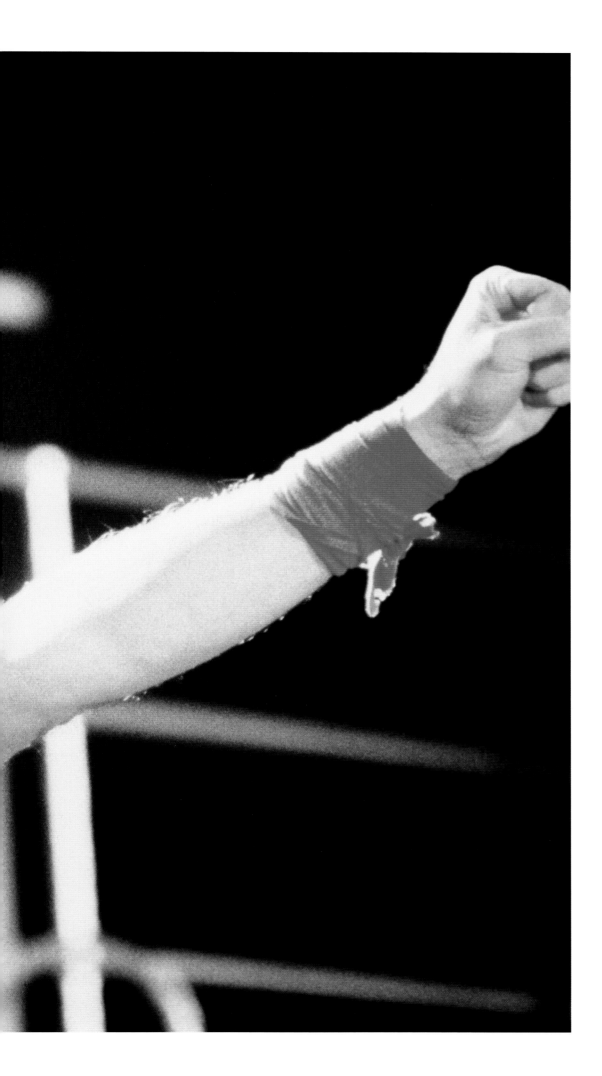

If 'I Want To Break Free' alienated some of Queen's audience, the video for 'Radio Ga Ga', made just months before in November 1983, must rate as having had a greater impact on Queen's audience than any other. Borrowing from and based heavily on Fritz Lang's Metropolis the rally crowd hand-clapping sequence became a trademark sight at Queen performances, never more dramatically on show than when Queen played Live Aid in 1985. Freddie in red leather trousers and crepe bandages, a macho world away from the Hoover and heels that were to follow.

"In the end, all the mistakes and all the excuses are down to me, I can't pass the buck."

The high camp element of Queen's 'I Want To Break Free' video was not confined to the sight of Freddie, Roger, Brian and John in stockings and skirts. Causing almost as much high dudgeon among the moral high ground was the ballet section featuring members of the Royal Ballet company. The sight of Freddie back in tights playing the pan pipes alienated most American States. Queen never toured the States again.

This costume designed by Diana Moseley for the 1984 'It's A Hard Life' video became known as 'The Prawn Outfit', not only because "the colour looked like a cooked prawn" says Peter Freestone, "but it also made him look like a giant prawn, especially with that hair. Roger and John didn't approve much either; you can see their disgust in the video as they walk across the stage muttering to each other. Freddie knew he looked ridiculous, but he didn't care, he wanted the whole thing to be totally over the top."

Perhaps one of Freddie's most enduring video characters
was his nod to Coronation Street's beloved Bet Lynch in
the dragged-up video for 'I Want To Break Free'.
Legend has it that as well as curling up on a sofa to watch
reruns of old classic Hollywood black and white films,
Freddie would occasionally tune into the nation's favourite
Street. Apart from some nifty work with a Hoover, one
of the most lasting impressions of Freddie's character
has to be those shocking pink earrings. "Bet always wore
loud earrings, so Freddie sent me out to find the loudest I
could. And you'll note they match the lipstick. Always the
perfectionist, Freddie."
Peter Freestone.

Having taken almost two years off from touring, Queen
returned in 1984 with The Works tour, which was to
see the band play only two UK cities, Birmingham and
London, although multiple dates in each city. The gigantic
set was based on the classic Fritz Lang film Metropolis,
which had also provided the inspiration for the 'Radio Ga
Ga' video. Apart from all other considerations, the UK
dates can be noted as the first time that Freddie wore his
'I Want To Break Free' boob and wig on stage, something
which went down a storm on home ground, but almost
caused riots when Freddie reprised the perfomance on stage
in South America.

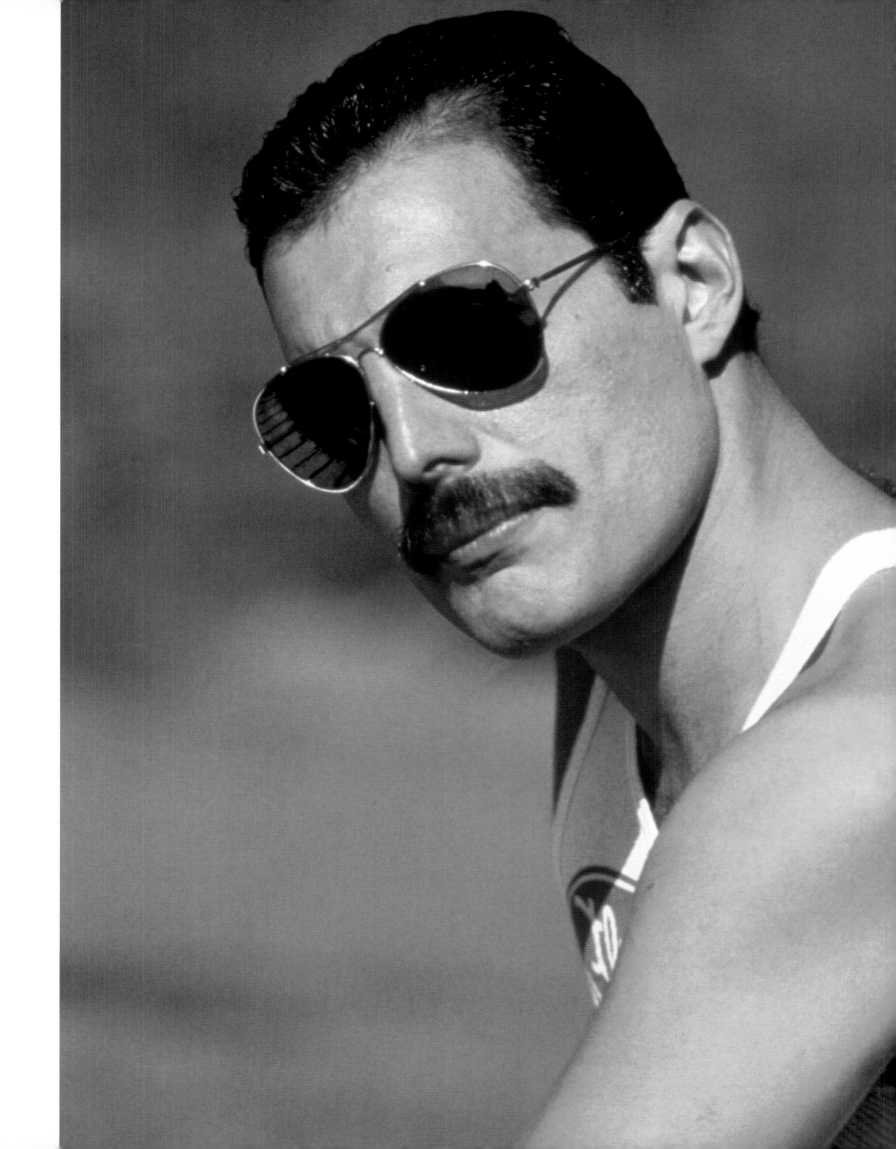

"I'm possessed by love. I'm a romantic … I think the songs on this album reflect my life; a diverse selection of moods," said Freddie of his first solo album, Mr Bad Guy, *released in 1984. This shot is a portrait from the suitably moody photo shoot for the album sleeve.*

Freddie rarely willingly appeared in print, but agreed to be one of five celebrities promoting diamonds for men in a Vogue *magazine supplement published on behalf of The Diamond Information Centre in the June 1984 edition. Freddie's chosen diamond pieces were a pair of black aluminium cufflinks set with one diamond designed by Roger Doyle and a gold and diamond signet ring by Cartier. The others celebrities featured were singer Lon Sutton, David Essex, Placido Domingo, and Billy Connolly. On his T-shirt Freddie wears a diamond and steel stud by Tom Dobbie.*

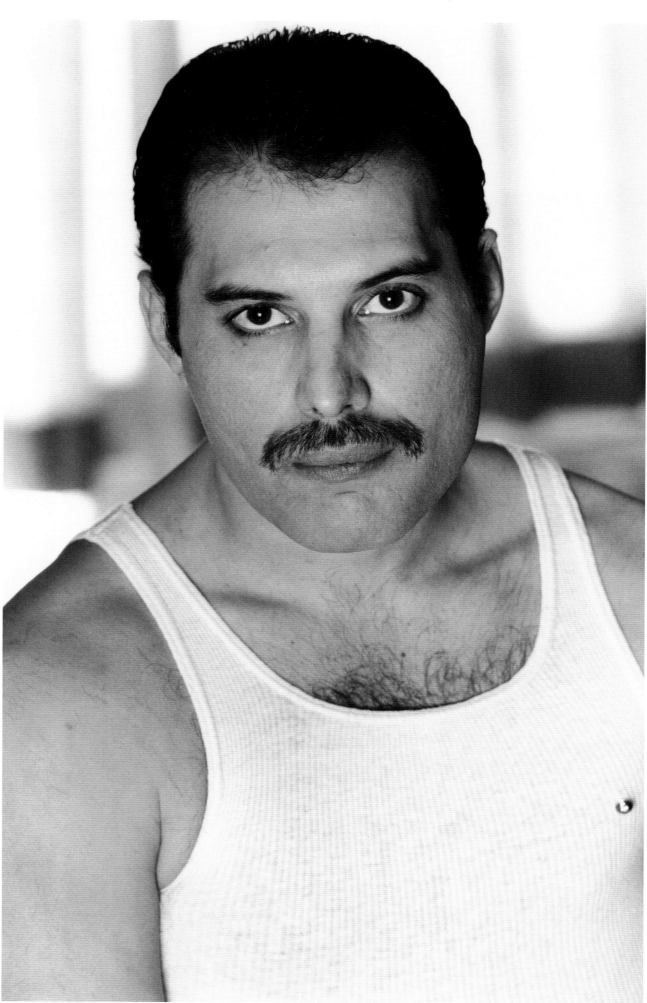

Having opened up South America to international music
artists, Queen triumphantly returned to open and close
the continent's first ever rock festival (Rock In Rio) – a
dozen top name artists performing over a period of ten
days to crowds that by Queen's final night had swollen to
a world record-breaking 300,000. Even torrential rain
and the inherent risk of using electrical powered equipment
in such conditions couldn't prevent Freddie and the band
from causing near hysteria among the massive crowd,
particularly when Freddie appeared on stage draped in the
Brazilian national flag at four o'clock in the morning.

Freddie's extended love affair with the city of Munich and all things Bavarian during the period 1984 to 1986 even began to be perceivable in the way he was dressing, as the Bavarian braces in this shot taken at Musicland studios in 1985 would seem to confirm. "He was very into the Bavarian lifestyle," says journalist David Wigg who was in Munich to interview Freddie when this picture was taken. "The only thing he didn't do was sing me The Sound of Music! *He liked Munich for the nightlife, the clubs and*

the restaurants. He found it a very invigorating city. He loved to fly friends over for dinner parties which he would give at his apartment. One of his great joys at that time was composing songs for the solo album he was recording. We were in the studio for hours, Freddie at the piano playing me the songs he had written for the album. He was very up and very happy – aided by lots of vodka between takes!"

By the mid-eighties Freddie had fallen out of love with New York. His new interest was Munich. Freddie got to know the city during the time Queen recorded The Works *album at Musicland Studios in 1984. It was the beginning of a new chapter in Freddie's life. While Queen took a short sabbatical, Freddie made a new circle of friends and began working on his first solo album,* Mr Bad Guy. *Ultimately Munich proved to be a fertile breeding ground of hits for both Queen and Freddie, including Freddie's 'Living On My Own'.*

Freddie's 39th birthday party at Mrs Hendersons, Munich, Germany, in September 1985 has become legendary. Freddie invited his closest friends to cross-dress and then filmed them for the video for his solo single, 'Living On My Own'. His record company protested and banned the video. In its full version it wasn't seen until the re-release of the track in August 1993. This is one of the tamer shots from that evening, Freddie and mystery guest.

'Dressed to kill' for his 39th birthday celebrations at Munich's Mrs Hendersons in September 1985, an evening that was to be captured in time in Freddie's 'Living On My Own' video.

"There's a voice inside me saying, 'Slow down Freddie, you're going to burn yourself out'. But I just can't stop."

For the video for his second solo single, 'I Was Born To Love You', Freddie returned to work with director David Mallet, a man familiar with, and always happy to indulge Freddie's taste for high camp. While the video begins in very simple fashion – with Freddie playing out a courtship scenario with an attractive young actress – it soon descends into mayhem, with 1,000 high-heeled, pink plastic-corseted amazonian dancers let loose on the studio floor. 'Pillow Talk meets Ride of the Valkyries', observed a junior production hand at the time!

"It came at exactly the right time, at a point where Freddie
was distinctly bored."
Peter Freestone.

"Freddie really didn't want to do it at first…but Geldof
was ringing us up on a daily basis and going 'come on boys
it's going to be the most wonderful thing'…and Bob is very
persuasive. He clobbered me, and he clobbered Roger – so
we both clobbered Fred, and Freddie went 'oh whatever,
okay' at some point. And we went on and the whole place
erupted. And we were dumbstruck and kinda humbled. I
think it galvanized us into going back into the studio and
believing in ourselves in a way we hadn't before."
Brian May.

"It was the perfect stage for Freddie: the world."
Bob Geldof.

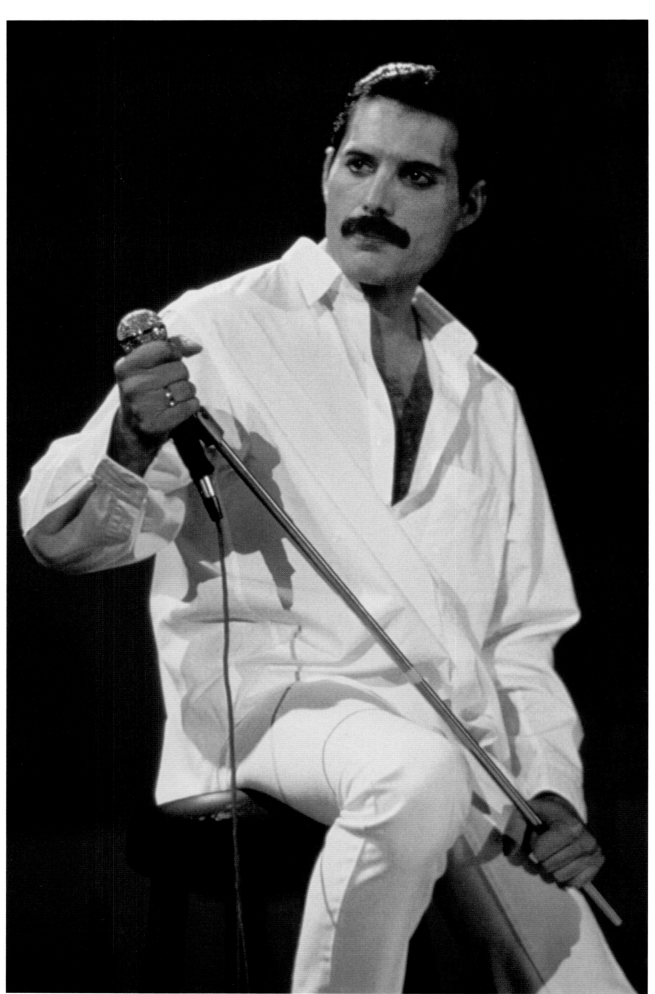

Many forget that Queen appeared not once, but twice at Live Aid. Having stolen the show earlier in the afternoon with a storming twenty-minute medley of hits, Freddie returned to the stage with Brian May just before the finale to perform an acoustic version of 'Is This The World We Created'. "We wrote this song long before the Live Aid project," said Freddie, "but everyone decided it fitted the occasion. It's about the unnecessary suffering and starvation among children around the world." Freddie admitted: "I can't watch TV film of Africa's starving millions. I have to switch off it disturbs me so much. Sometimes I do feel helpless, and this is one of those times I can do my bit."

Above, right and previous page: Freddie's fascination with ballet and opera and the effects of his regular visits to Covent Garden had a marked impression on several videos he and the band filmed in the mid-eighties; 'I Want to Break Free' and 'It's A Hard Life', particularly. But in none were these influences so pronounced as in the video for 'Made In Heaven', his third single, released in June 1985. Here, a London warehouse was transformed into a replica of the London Opera House proscenium stage. Freddie's references were two ballets, Stravinsky's The Rite of Spring *and Dante's* Inferno. *Once again in the hands of video visionary David Mallet, Freddie and a huge cast created an extraordinary classical production, culminating with Freddie as 'the king of the world', positioned some 60 feet above the ground, and suffering a bad case of vertigo. David Mallet recalls:*

"I wouldn't have gone up there, and I don't think half the riggers would have done either. In the end, to get him through it, we had to wire him up. But it was Fred's idea in the first place!"

By 1986 when Queen came to film the video for 'Princes of the Universe' from the film Highlander, *the shoots had taken on cinematic proportions. To create one of the climactic scenes from the film, the band took over the largest sound stage at London's Elstree Studios, hired the actual star of the film, Christophe Lambert to star opposite Freddie, and reconstructed the rooftop to-the-death duelling scene. "Freddie and Christophe struck it off well," recalls Peter Hince, "but otherwise he appeared less than impressed. For Freddie it was just another video day, a very long day, and it was bloody cold... I remember mostly Freddie complaining about how cold it was. Freddie always hated the cold."*

*Freddie returned to the stage he had so commanded at
Live Aid the previous year – London's Wembley Stadium
– for two nights in mid-July 1986. The shows heralded the
imminent end of the UK leg of Queen's A Kind of Magic
tour (although Knebworth would be hastily added as the
final closure). For Freddie, who was looking forward to
returning to the setting of his Live Aid triumph, it was a
major celebration; friends were flown in from New York
and a specially hired coach ferried guests from his proud
new Garden Lodge home to Wembley. It was, according
to personal assistant Peter Freestone, "the start of one very
long party. That day must have been one of the happiest
of his life."*

*OVERLEAF: "I don't think anyone expected the Magic
Tour to be the band's last dates; things had gone so well we
were already planning the next one," says Gerry Stickells,
Queen's tour manager. "Live Aid had totally regenerated
the band, both in terms of their audience and their
attitude. There was no sense of anything coming to an end
after the second Wembley show, the band were off to a
party at Kensington Roof Gardens," (another which went
down in history, mostly for the naked, body-painted lift
attendants) " and the mood was very up."*

On July 27, 1986 Queen broke new ground by playing the first ever open air stadium rock concert behind the Iron Curtain in Budapest before a sell-out audience of 80,000 at the Nepstadion (The People's Stadium). Ticket demands for the event were over-subscribed by a quarter of a million.

A month later Queen were to play their last ever concert. Freddie's weariness with the pressures of touring were beginning to show. Backstage after the record-breaking stadium concert he told journalist David Wigg: "It takes a strong-willed person to survive. You have to be one step ahead all the time. You have to be so astute, so strong. You have to be a hard faced bitch – and a lot of us can't be."

On the eve of what were to be his last ever UK dates, Freddie photographed backstage at Slane Castle in Dublin, on 5 July, 1986. Queen would then play Newcastle, London, Manchester and their final performance at Knebworth Park on August 9. Photographer Richard Young, who by this time had become a member of Freddie's trusted inner circle, recalls that Freddie was in a particularly playful mood that day. "Freddie was sitting outside his trailer; he was in a kind of mischievous mood. I just said, 'Freddie where's your crown?' He rushed into his trailer where it was and popped it on his head. I think that smile says a lot about how he was that day."

'Who Wants To Live Forever' video, September 1986.
"I certainly don't have any aspirations to live to 70 … it
would be boring."
Freddie.

A final bow. Freddie's last appearance on stage,
Knebworth, August 9, 1986, the end of The Magic
Tour. "I don't think a forty-two-year-old man should
be running around in his leotard any more. It's not very
becoming." It's probably more the truth that Freddie knew
he was losing the strength such gruelling touring schedules
demanded.

"I'm not going to be one of those old hams that keeps going on and on. I'd rather leave it at the top."

It took ten hours being trapped in the band's sound delay tower for photographer Richard Gray to capture the absolute final moment on stage when Freddie raised his crown for the last time.

"At the end of the Magic Tour, the biggest tour we've ever done, Freddie said 'I don't want to do this any more.' It was kind of uncharacteristic because he was always up for everything and very strong, very optimistic. The fact that he was quite definite about the fact that he didn't want to do it was something different. We thought maybe it's just a stage he's going through, or maybe there's something wrong. I remember having that thought in my head, but you push that thought aside."
Brian May.

At the end of 1986 Freddie wrote in his Christmas letter to the Queen fan club: "The tour was fun and a great success although I must admit I had to be coaxed into doing it. I'm glad I did it now. The band are now working on the Budapest Live Show to be out on video in early 1987. I'm also working on a solo project – it's so secretive even I don't know what it's about ... Take care. Lots of love..."

Little could match Freddie's previous birthday party, his black and white cross-dressing ball at Munich's Mrs Hendersons, but his 40th, held at home at Garden Lodge in London was a heady affair, a royal garden party. This shot, taken September 1986 shows a collection of the hats as worn by guests Peter Freestone, Jim Hutton, Joe Fanelli, Jim and Claudia Beach, Mary Austin, and Peter Straker. As Freddie was often prompted to remark: "Very fetching my dears."

Taking time off from a shopping expedition in Tokyo during the 1986 Magic Tour. On one such shopping trip in Japan the media claimed Freddie spent a million pounds.

"I've stopped having sex and started growing tulips."

"I'd like to be buried with all my treasures, just like the Pharaohs. If I could afford it, I'd have a pyramid built in Kensington."

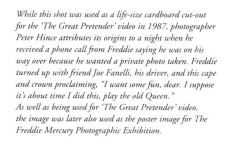

While this shot was used as a life-size cardboard cut-out for the 'The Great Pretender' video in 1987, photographer Peter Hince attributes its origins to a night when he received a phone call from Freddie saying he was on his way over because he wanted a private photo taken. Freddie turned up with friend Joe Fanelli, his driver, and this cape and crown proclaiming, "I want some fun, dear. I suppose it's about time I did this, play the old Queen."
As well as being used for 'The Great Pretender' video, the image was later also used as the poster image for The Freddie Mercury Photographic Exhibition.

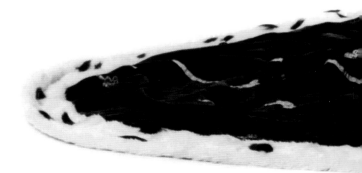

Freddie in what became known as 'the snooker outfit', taken in 1986 by Peter Hince. "Freddie was very into tuxedos and bow ties by this time. He said it was to do with getting old and calming down, but we called it the Barcelona effect, the influence of working with Montserrat Caballé." Freddie's personal favourite portrait, it later was used for the cover of The Freddie Mercury Album.

"Why 'The Great Pretender'? Because I AM The Great Pretender!"
Freddie's cover version of the classic The Platters' 1956 hit gave him a top five solo hit and a chance to re-visit some of his favourite characters as portrayed in a decades worth of Queen videos. Now, who could he be pretending to be in this shot from the 1987 video shoot?

"I think The Great Pretender is a great
title for what I do."

Freddie in the glowing pink suit designed for him for 'The Great Pretender' video by David Chambers, who also made a number of Freddie's other suits including the dark blue tuxedo worn in the 'Barcelona' video. This was not the original colour Chambers had in mind for Freddie. According to photographer Peter Hince, when Freddie tried on the suit for the first time he preferred the colour of the lining and had the suit remade out of the lining fabric.

It is unlikely that anyone but Freddie would have the persuasive power to get Queen's Roger Taylor back into women's clothing for a second time after their collective drag appearance in the 'I Want To Break Free' video. Here's the proof, the backing singers from 'The Great Pretender' video, 1987. Freddie, by the way, is the one on the left. The mystery 'girl' in the centre is actor Peter Straker, one of Freddie closest friends.

During a television interview in Spain in July 1986
Freddie talked of his love of opera and in particular singer
Montserrat Caballé. His words did not go unheard. Nine
months later Freddie was in the studio with Montserrat
recording 'Barcelona', a song that has become an
anthem worldwide. The Olympian-scale video brought
them together to film in one of the biggest film stages at
Pinewood Studios, summer 1987.

Montserrat Caballé: "Barcelona was an example of the high musical talent of Freddie. He was not only a popular singer, he was a musician, that could sit at the piano and compose for me. He discovered a new way to bring music together. He was the first and only person that has done this." Barcelona video, 1987.
This portrait, taken during the filming, is his mother Jer's favourite.

From the start of the recording of the 'Barcelona' album in April 1987 throughout the rest of his life, Freddie shared a special friendship with opera diva Montserrat Caballé. His affection for her shows in this warm portrait taken during the photo session for their album.

By the time Queen came to film the video for 'I'm Going Slightly Mad' in February 1991 the outward signs of Freddie's illness were becoming increasingly obvious. His idea for disguising his appearance was an outrageous wig, heavy white make-up and to shoot in black and white, a concept that was inspired by silent movies and mime artists. At the time Freddie expected this to be the last video he would shoot.

'These Are The Days of Our Lives', made in May 1991, was the final video in which Freddie appeared. Freddie's frail health is evident not only in his appearance, but in the fact that he unusually stands still throughout. Peter Freestone recalls that by this time it was sheer agony for Freddie to walk. During the latter period of Freddie's poor health only one person was trusted to photograph him, the band's art director Richard Gray who took this picture during filming.

In it Freddie wears his favourite waistcoat, a present from a friend who had had it specially painted with pictures of Freddie's six cats. This shot remains the last portrait to be taken of him.

Jimi Hendrix.

Rock Hudson.

Freddie's sister, Kash.

Psychedelia.

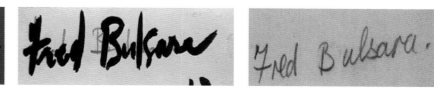

*Examples of work done by Freddie at
Ealing College of Art.*

I was Born to Love You
With every single beat of my Heart
I was Born to take care of
Every single day of my life

You were Made for me
I was waiting for you
It was a matter of time
There was a place in

I lead the same old

Born Born
E5 C#
A6 G6+
C# B6+
E6

You could dance
I would kill

I wanna here
I Love every
I wanna here
Born to Love

FRED PARADISE FOR MAN
for something

F A
F A C B6 x2
F A
A C Bb F
A
A C Bb C
Bb
Bb C
G C Em F
Bb6 G Dm
x2

D D D
G6 D F G
G Amp
F# A F# Esus
E# E C# x2
G U Gsus
RUN

More to life Than This

Cope
without Love,
these Broken Hearts
to these Crying Faces

See More to Life How Thinking
See More Than Meets the Eye
And Hope
Mind to Life Than This
Peace See More
must be
Lord So full of Hate
Everywhere
create

love is no square deal
love don't give no justification
Love It strikes like cold steel
Love Kills
love can
Play with your emotion
It's an open invitation
to your heart
(Kills) 2
Living Part time
Burning Your life time
Gives You
it and time
to go

Love Kills to the bone
Love drills your heart
Love chills you to the bone
Love restless your slave
That's no indication
Station
When love becomes the
And you take to drink

münchen
hilton
Am Tucherpark 7
8000 München 22
Tel. (089) 34 00 51
Telegramme Hiltels
Telex 05 215 740

EUROCARD · MASTER CARD · ACCESS
WILLKOMMEN · ALWAYS WELCOME · BIENVENUE
BANK ODER SPARKASSE NACH EUROCARD

love don't give no compensation
love don't pay no bills
2'30
love don't give no indication
(love just won't) stand still
Love Kills
Drills you thru your heart
Love Kills
Scars you from the start
It's just a living pastime
Ruling your heart time
Ruling your lifetime
Stay for a lifetime
it just won't let go
Love
won't leave you alone

Everybody
Everybody was
Everybody

Anybody knows
A readymade plan of how to succeed
Then a devil in my path
escape

A lot of people on the go are going
worked out fast
body is talking tension
people on the
an

Love or Dangerous
Made in Heaven
let's turn it on
Living on my own
Foolin Around

There must be more to life R
Mr Bad Guy
Your kind of lover
Man Made Paradise

love makin love TV/me R
Stop all the fighting R
love me like TV/me

Love Kills

28 days left

6 days mixing
Block I

22 days left
6 days
Block II

18 days left

Mr Block II 5 days
13 days left

Block III 14 days
—1 left
Existing 1 Day
—2 Days left

1/4
7/4
G
G
Gm
Gm7
Gm
Gm7
Gm
Eb
Gm
Eb
Eb
F

body is taking tension
people on the move
big problem fast

See Everyday you wear
a different Face
to make a living for the
rest of your life

Man Made Pa Ra Dise
F#6 Abdt F# Bbdt
Abdt Bbdt Eb D E
C# D Eb

You think you couldn't get higher
(its squeezing you deeper now)
love caught in the crossfire
love just won't let you
love won't leave you

Only
the One for Me
the Man for You
were Made for Me
My Extacy
If I was given Every Opportunity
I'd kill for Your love
So Take a Chance with
Let me Romance
I'm Just Caught in a
dream and my dream
true
had to believe
in Feel

FOOLING AROUND

you're so beautiful, you just lay it on me
foxy lady, you really are the greatest show
you want to play
you wanna eat your cake and have it your way
got it easy and you don't give a damn
fooling around, you just keep fooling around

Walking down the street, people watching closely
you're a tease, you can turn on any man you want
masquerade, you catch of the season every night
fooling, you don't have any time for me
you just keep fooling around with me

fooling around — everywhere I go you are the only
fooling around, all you do is keep me hanging around
you're really so hard to please
you gotta really watch that, baby

I wanna play, but you always want it all your own way
fooling around, you just keep fooling around with me
fool, fool for you baby, keep fooling around
fool, fool for you sexy baby, keep fooling a
fool, fool for you baby, keep fooling around

words and music : FREDDIE ME

You just — fooling around
you just fooling around
fooling — you keep fooling
fooling — fooling fooling

Your the one for me
I am the man for you
You were made for me
You're my day extacy
If I was given every opportunity
I would kill for your love
mad

love chills
love kills
it stops freezes you in time

F F A C
F F A C Bb F
F F A C Bb C
D
stop 4. G K
G ADK
D
G6D
G6D x2
C K C K C G6m
C G
Eb B C
Eb

PICTURE CREDITS